POLITICAL
BLIND SPOTS

POLITICAL BLIND SPOTS

Reading the Ideology of Images

Raphael Sassower and Louis Cicotello

LEXINGTON BOOKS

A division of
ROWMAN & LITTLEFIELD PUBLISHERS, INC.
Lanham • Boulder • New York • Toronto • Oxford

LEXINGTON BOOKS

A division of Rowman & Littlefield Publishers, Inc.
A wholly owned subsidiary of The Rowman & Littlefield Publishing Group, Inc.
4501 Forbes Boulevard, Suite 200
Lanham, MD 20706

PO Box 317
Oxford
OX2 9RU, UK

British Library Cataloguing in Publication Information Available

Library of Congress Cataloging-in-Publication Data

Sassower, Raphael.
  Political blind spots : reading the ideology of images / Raphael Sassower and
Louis Cicotello.
        p. cm.
  Includes bibliographical references and index.
  ISBN 0-7391-1137-X (cloth : alk. paper)—ISBN 0-7391-1261-9 (pbk. : alk.
paper)
  Cloth 13: 978-0-7391-1137-6
  Paper 13: 978-0-7391-1261-8
1. Art—Political aspects.   2. Aesthetics—Political aspects.   3. Art and society.
4. Art, Modern—20th century.   I. Cicotello, Louis, 1940-   II. Title.
N72.P6S27 2005
701'.03—dc22   2005027298

Printed in the United States of America

♾™ The paper used in this publication meets the minimum requirements of
American National Standard for Information Sciences—Permanence of Paper
for Printed Library Materials, ANSI/NISO Z39.48-1992.

Dedicated to the memory of all those who
died or suffered because of
ideological zeal and visual manipulation.

CONTENTS

LIST OF ILLUSTRATIONS

PREFACE

On some level, everything is political in the sense of being open to an interpretation that is political in nature that belies a political view or commitment.

When one of us goes on a hiking trip to the valleys of Utah, rather than stay in our fair city along the front range of Colorado and walk along a major commercial boulevard, we appreciate the desire to be in nature and observe its pastoral beauty. But what is at stake here? Is it the exercise? Probably not, since a walk along a busy metropolitan boulevard is just as long and arduous. Is it the views? Probably not, since the mountain range in both cases are similarly spectacular. Instead, the great state of Utah, with its commerce department and tourism bureau, its governor's office and its chamber of commerce, all colluded to sell its natural beauty to unsuspecting tourists and hikers, bicyclists and campers: the message is clearly sent with pictures and photographs, posters and websites, invitations and solicitations. The great state of Utah doesn't reveal its peculiar position as the headquarters of a religious sect that promotes polygamy and denies alcohol consumption, because this might deter tourists. Instead, the wholesome image it portrays is devoid of religious advocacy or political flair: look at our natural beauty, it says, and not at the policies we have enacted. A similar situation can be perceived in states, such as California and New York, that have attracted domestic and international tourists because of the self-images they have constructed over the years, regardless of their political realities. For example, one would not associate either state with a great military-industrial complex, but rather think of the great cultural and artistic centers they have become. Beaches come to mind in the case of California and not factories that emit pollution to the ocean; refined tastes and fashion come to mind in the case of New York and not the illegal immigrants who toil to make them possible or the underground economy that is as powerful as Wall Street. All of these cases remind us of the predicament of artistic portraits of political messages: Is what you see as a staged image indeed the reality or the ideas that gave rise to it? If distortion and manipulation are inherent in image production, how would a viewer ever uncover the "truth" of the message? Moreover, is there indeed a truth there to be revealed? If yes, whose truth is it anyway?

We designed this book as a sequel to our previous one on art, commerce, and technoscience (Sassower and Cicotello 2000) as intricate and mutually influential factors and realities in the development of art in the past century. For us, the European and American avant-garde artists exemplified a precarious line one had to stride between full complicity with the forces of commerce and the technological advances of the era (at least in the sense of mass and popular culture) and outright critique of anything financial and industrial. We attribute the success of some of the artists in the twentieth century to what we termed detached engagement, a way of making the best use they could of the available elements in their culture without losing their sense of integrity and creativity. Our present effort is similar in approach, but adds a focus on audience reception of political institutions, such as the state.

We revisit the twentieth century since it provides a fertile ground from which to cull numerous European and American examples of detached engagement, with concerns for survival, on the one hand, and outright profiteering and political complicity on the other. Our focus this time is on art, politics, and propaganda, namely, an examination of the visual means by which ideological convictions and promises find their popular expression. As we have seen in the previous book, the lines of demarcation between high and low art, between the fine and popular arts, have been blurred in the twentieth century. This means that we can more readily examine posters and billboards as artistic embodiment of ideals and ideas, and not merely as cheap devices by which commercial interests sell their wares. Moreover, the aesthetic appeal that these media have is mass appeal; hence, it's something useful for economic exploitation. The exploitation, in turn, transcends the economic area into the political (and obviously the two are interrelated).

When we get into the political use of aesthetics, when we examine the specific cases of overtly politicized artworks, we find something counterintuitive: regardless of diverse ideologies, the artworks are almost identical. Totalitarian regimes, sometimes understood to be fascist in nature, seem to use the same visual vocabulary and grammar as democratic ones. This is fascinating in itself, for it has been repeatedly the case during the past century that these regimes fought each other using the same aesthetic tools. Was this the case because of their visual appeal for domestic consumption only? Was it because they learned from each other what was the most effective way of mobilizing their people to fight wars? However one answers these questions (which we don't), it's still an amazing phenomenon that fascists and anti-fascists alike make an appeal to the same images.

But there is a related point we'd like to make in this context. Noticing the images employed by fascists and democrats is not simply saying that they use similar or identical aesthetic tools, such as color schemes and posters, but suggesting that they appeal to similar if not identical archetypical ideas, as anthropologists or cultural psychologists (Carl Jung, for one) might call them. If this is the case, as we demonstrate, and without adhering to some reductionist view that "it's all in the genes," does this mean that there is no such a thing as national identity that is sufficiently different from one country to another? Does this, then, mean that there is a universal vocabulary and grammar for art with some biological or organic roots? We return here to the classical debate between relativism and universalism, modernism and postmodernism, reductionism and complexity, between those who identify and classify cultural difference and those who find common human threads among all the differences. Can aesthetics have it both ways? Can you identify some underlying principles of aesthetic perception, or are you limited by the cultural cues that determine how one reads aesthetics?

Though our focus is on aesthetics, it should be clear from the outset that similar questions can be raised in regard to ideology itself as an intellectual framework against which political agendas and policies respectively are developed and implemented. That is, can we say that regardless if you espouse communism or democracy, you will be concerned with freedom and equality, courage and honesty, heroism and diligence? Yes, you may transform the terms and ideas a bit and speak of absolute versus relative equality, absolute versus circumscribed freedom, and so on. But aren't we all dreaming about and fighting for freedom? What regime says outright that it's against freedom? Now freedom can be explained in many ways, and the focus can shift from the individual to the community and back again; but these are means to an end, not the ends themselves about which we might find disagreements. So, are there universal, rather than culturally specific, ideals? We have a long tradition in the western history of ideas of different answers to these questions, and we plan not to rehearse them here. Suffice here to say that regardless of the diverse answers, the visual representation of these ideals (and answers) has found a common ground that is our focus.

Since our focus is on the visual representation of political ideals (ideology in this sense), we are interested in how they are read by the public. It is interesting that the intent of political leaders and party officials and the ways in which they are communicated to the artists, and furthermore the way the artists communicate these ideals visually in turn, cannot control the message. That is, by the time an image is portrayed, it takes on a life of its own, it becomes detached from the original intent of the creator and the ones who commissioned it. If it's open to interpretation, can it still convey the message originally intended? If not, what use does it have? Here is where the art of propaganda comes into play as a direct message machine that is supposed to be clear and succinct, direct and unequivocal. Under these conditions, then, the politician must rely on the artist to do the right thing, to reach the public, to ensure that the intent isn't lost, and that the right results will ensue (enlist farmers to the military, ensure hard work with little reward for the glory of the state, and the like). The artwork becomes an essential tool of the authorities.

The artist, then, is the conduit for political expression and control, the one who must decide whether to be complicit in influencing the public to believe in a particular ideology or be a critic who can oppose the authorities. Complicity under capitalist democracy seems benign as compared to complicity under fascism. But, structurally and literally, there is no difference at all. In both cases, the artist uses aesthetic devices to convince and cajole a confused and skeptical public of the right thing to do, how to think and behave, following the prescription of powerful elites with agendas and goals, with blueprints from which no one should deviate.

THE ARTISTIC PREDICAMENT OF IDEOLOGICAL COMPLICITY

I: THE ENDS OF IDEOLOGY

We should admit from the outset that aesthetic expression is an expression of something, a viewpoint, an idea, a taste. As such, artists don't work in an intellectual vacuum, no mater how loath they are to discuss their *ideas* or their *ideological commitments*. Moreover, whatever is produced and labeled as works of art is undertaken within a certain economic, social, and political context that becomes clear once analysis is allowed. This critical perspective has become evident to the public since John Berger, for example, delivered a series of lectures with accompanying visual representations on BBC (eventually turned into a best-selling book). In it, Berger argues convincingly that even the oil paintings of the Renaissance embodied a bourgeois conviction not only because of the subject matter and the particular expensive medium in which it was delivered, but that a whole set of material conditions and ideological prejudices went into this process of aesthetic consumption. For example, Berger focuses on the male gaze of nude female images as a way of objectifying them and possessing them in one's private chambers. In going through this analysis, Berger shifts art history and art appreciation into a lesson in the politics of aesthetics uncovering (or revealing) or the ideological foundation against which judgment and choice must be made.

Ingres's highly detailed oil painting *The Grande Odalisque*, featuring a nude female sumptuously on display for male pleasure, is exactly an image of consumption that Berger points to in his critique. Illustration 4, the Guerrilla Girls' poster *Do Women have to be naked to get into the Met. Museum?* of 1989, draws on the fine art of Ingres's nude as a source for its composition as a strategy typical of many advertising images. The Guerrilla Girls' art makes a witty reversal of the politics of those kinds of images as their text from a feminist viewpoint. They mock the exclusive domains of museums and galleries, where male gatekeepers wish to interact with women only as objectified nude images readily available for consumption. More specifically, the posters were displayed on walls outside the museum only to remind the public that their own posters and flyers and other graphic materials were excluded from a show of political posters called "Committed to Print" at the Museum of Modern Art, ironically on the grounds that what they did wasn't "art" but "politics," (Timmers 1998–99). The Guerrilla Girls fight the sexism and racism that dominate the art world, and they have been punished for their outspoken critique, as for example, when their poster (listed above) that was originally intended to be part of a billboard series sponsored by the Public Art Fund in New York City was eventually rejected. It was subsequently self-funded for public display on buses and streets by this anonymous group of women artists.

If art cannot be exempt from its political underpinnings, as Berger suggests, and if every aesthetic judgment embodies an ideological commitment, then it might be prudent to figure out first what we mean by ideology, second how that meaning or meanings are related to the art world, and third, how to examine the role of artists within this framework. We will begin with our answers to these issues, and then go into detail about the intellectual background that allows us to conclude the way we do. First, by ideology we mean both the conservative view of Daniel Bell who speaks of the "end of [Marxist] ideology" and the leftist/Marxist view of Terry Eagleton who speaks of the sociological interpretation of the relationship between theory and practice. Second, we continue from Eagleton's position and (contrary to him) emphasize how aesthetic elements of our contemporary cultures are essential not as expressions of ideologies but as ways to even comprehend what these ideologies are all about. Thus, we reverse the focus from the ideology of aesthetics to the aesthetics of ideologies. And third, we argue that artists, as producers and (in some cases) distributors of aesthetic objects have the inevitable predicament of complicity and critical dissent.

It's important to consider the various interpretations of the term *ideology*. For Daniel Bell, there is a specific context to the notion of ideology, namely, the period between the 1930s and the 1950s. In that period, one has seen the assent of Marxist ideas in their peculiar application in the communist ideals of the Soviet Union, and the descent of Fascist ideology into the horrors of Stalin's gulags, Hitler's concentration camps, and Mussolini's authoritative bureaucracy. In all these cases, great ideas and ideals, such as the pursuit of individual happiness within a community of free and equal laborers, for example, have become an excuse for establishing power relations and abuse of power. The Communist Party expanded its powers and dictated the material conditions under which every citizen worked, so that, for Bell, "the end of ideology" is the demise of the lofty ideals by which one should pursue one's life—the promise and hope have turned into a nightmare, or what Bell terms "the exhaustion of political ideas in the fifties." As he says, "For ideology, which once was a road to action, has come to be a dead end" (Bell 1961, 393), In this case, the ideas were bankrupt and the road to their accomplishment was destroyed; hence, communism as an ideology has become a dead end. Since "ideology was linked to philosophical idealism" (395), and since the conditions of the Soviet Union claimed a "universal validity" in the name of a particular "class interest" (396) in the sense of the concentration of power in the hands a few politburo functionaries, it was obvious that this road to nirvana was obsolete.

Bell's indictment against the leftist, Soviet-dominated view of ideology can be summarized in this way:

> But in popular usage the word *ideology* remains as a vague term where it seems to denote a world-view or belief-system or creeds held by a social group about the social arrangements in society, which is morally justified as being right. (399)

Ideology, then, is a "secular religion" (400) with a passion that ends up justifying a particular view as the ideal or foundation for particular social "arrangements" that end up legitimating structures and power relations that otherwise would be suspect. It's the moral authority (supposed or seemingly inherent) that bothers Bell more than anything else, and therefore he finds parallels in the ideological debates that have a political bent to those of religious fanatics; it's the moral pretense that upsets his intellectual sensibility. So, ideological motivations are suspect, ideological decrees are outright misrepresentations, and ideological musings are meant to confuse and subdue. Finally, in the name of ideology individual rights and responsibilities seem to be truncated and oppressed, deemed an inconvenience on the road to freedom.

On the other end of the ideological spectrum, there is the actual Marxist defense of ideological commitment that brings about change. On some level, Terry Eagleton doesn't seem to disagree with Daniel Bell's assessment, even though he ends up at a different solution to the problems associated with the Soviet Union's misuse of Marx's ideals. For him, though, the culprit is the postmodern theoretical framework in which any set of ideas or ideals is undermined and found to be wanting (Eagleton 1991, xi). He then proceeds to outline some fifteen different meanings associated with the term *ideology*, so as to highlight the ambiguity of having a single definition. The most useful definition for our purposes is "ideas which help to legitimate a dominant political power" (1). In using this definition, the notion of "false ideas" or "false consciousness," to continue the Marxist critique of ideology, is set aside in order to appreciate the need for political powers to legitimate themselves, find a way to argue that their views are correct and worth pursuing (sometimes at any cost).

Ideology in this sense is a useful term for Eagleton to suggest that "central" social issues and beliefs can more clearly be argued about if they come under the rubric of ideology than if they are merely construed as a set of policies or caprice of the authorities. Eagleton is sensitive, along Berger's lines of argument, to the linguistic elements that determine our beliefs and our views of meaning and truth. They both agree with Nelson Goodman (1976) that art has its own languages that we learn to interpret. Once we relinquish the standard notion of meaning as a mirror-reflection of what nature reveals (in the sense of Wittgenstein's *Tractatus* of 1922), and appreciate the complexity of meanings we ourselves impose on what we see and how we learn to communicate what we see (in the sense of Wittgenstein's *Philosophical Investigations* of 1958), then it makes sense to speak of ideology the way both Berger and Eagleton do. For them, ideas and beliefs, ideals and moral convictions, find their way into our vocabulary (both linguistic and visual) so that they inform what we see and how we interpret how we see.

Our visual world, then, isn't simply the "naked" or the "innocent" eye observing nature and its various artistic depictions, but in fact a view filtered through a process of learning (and indoctrination) that socializes us in particular ways, that offers us a set of meanings we attach to our perception; hence the importance of "ideology." So, whether we like it or not, claims Eagleton, we must deal with epistemological questions, namely, the ways in which we accumulate and communicate knowledge claims; it's not as easy as it seems, yet, it is easy enough to recognize once alerted to it (Eagleton 1991, 22–3). In the case of aesthetics, he argues that "the very language which elevates art offers perpetually to undermine it." The languages of art, then, are transformed once the big term *aesthetics* is brought forth: it provides a level of abstraction and a level of formalized discourse that carries it away from the particular art pieces under consideration in everyday experiences (Eagleton 1990, 2–3). Eagleton then continues to argue that though aesthetics is commonly understood by the left to be a "bourgeois concept," it doesn't follow from this that it's necessarily worthy of condemnation rather than analysis. For him, a proper dialectical approach could illuminate the emancipatory power of aesthetics, the potential it carries, because of (and not despite) its political undertones in relation to the material processes that are already under way to provide personal edification and liberation from the clutches of capitalism and consumerism (8–9, 351).

We take our cues from these scholars in order to move on with our own discussion. We agree that ideology plays a role in the conception and expression of aesthetic objects. We agree that one can trace an ideological commitment in particular works of art. And we likewise agree that it's important not to gloss over these connections between art and politics, between artworks and their popular appeal (in light of an idea or belief), between the languages of art and propaganda. And what is that difference to us? It's one thing to say that artists express or re-present reality, and quite another to admit that they inherently take a position in doing so (since they interpret in the process of re-presenting). Here is another way of articulating this way of thinking, this critical process of viewing our world. We could start with the way we live our lives, the way we relate to each other, the way our education and career are set, and the ways in which we are rewarded for our accomplishments. In order to organize and explain and eventually legitimate this state of affairs we deploy a framework, a set of ideas, an ideology. If you buy into this ideology, accept that this framework makes sense; you'll be able to explain to yourself and others the particular situation or set of circumstances in which you find yourself. But in order to make this move, this shift from your reality to a set of ideas that justify it and make sense of it, you need props. The props, so to speak, are visual aids, visual devices with which this shift can move more smoothly mentally, cognitively, psychologically, and emotionally.

In fact, those visual tools and mechanisms, posters and commercials, advertisements and monuments, end up being more central to our process of self-legitimization and self-realization than we wish to admit. What we mean by this is the manner in which a visual representation on an idea, such as the *Statue of Liberty* or the *Vietnam War Veterans' Memorial*, becomes a substitute of sort for any verbalization and linguistic communication of any idea under the sun. We don't need to use words, such as freedom and heroism, liberty and courage, respectively, in order to understand why we volunteer to serve our country, why we welcome immigrants (or not), believe in equality and integration, endorse policies that ensure the well-being of all citizens and expect our country to protect our rights and safety. Yes, a symbol or visual cue can speak a thousand words; yes, it can have a more powerful impact than any lecture at a university or any learned treatise. So, if this is the case, then we should acknowledge and study the centrality of the visual medium as a legitimation instrument of ideological commitments and their manifestation in everyday life (see illustrations 1 and 2, where American and French patriotism are set next to each other, supposedly featuring similar ideological commitments to freedom, equality, and humanity or fraternity).

The way we move forward in this discussion is to highlight some interesting themes along this path. The first and foremost is that predicament of artists in the process of producing and distributing artworks (Chapter 1). The second is the problematic framing of ideologies (democracy and totalitarianism) using similar (sometimes identical) images (Chapter 2). And the third is the quandary of conveying a national identity (an ideology of sorts) that turns out to have a universal appeal (Chapters 3–4).

II: THE IDEOLOGY OF THE AVANT-GARDE

Though we are building on Eagleton's insights, we should emphasize that our ultimate interest is in reversing his "the ideology of the aesthetics" into the aesthetics of ideology (in Chapter 2), namely, the ways in which art ends up delivering ideological messages, whether intended or not. In order to fill some of the background related to this suggestion, we'll refer to our earlier manuscript that dealt with twentieth-century avant-garde artists (in Europe and the United States of America) and the kind of predicaments they faced (Sassower and Cicotello 2000). We argued that their predicament was in part because of the position of the community of artists within a broader cultural matrix, one that was infused with capitalist "ideology" and practice as well as with the latest advances of science and technology. We explained the particular prominence some of these artists held in the public's eye because of their detached engagement. In a way, we wanted to explain and illustrate our concerns and insights through a re-examination of a particular time line, namely, the twentieth century.

Detached engagement, for us, was a term that could explain the artists' predicament on the one hand, and their coping strategy on the other. Though acquiring a celebrity status, like Andy Warhol, and enjoying the limelight and all the financial rewards that come with such a status, they were also crafty and clever critics of the culture in which they lived, like Marcel Duchamp. They walked a tightrope between assailing their culture and its consumerist mentality, while producing consumable products that sold for millions of dollars, such as Yves Klein and Keith Haring. Is there a contradiction here? Not really, from our perspective. Instead, we believe that being adept at the changing conditions of one's surroundings makes an artist (and not only a businessperson or a politician) a more effective communicator of ideas and expressions. Instead of the nostalgia of the creative individual whose isolation and separation from the affairs of the state, a kind of romantic or religious asceticism, enhances her vision and depth of depiction, we offer a view of the artist as enmeshed in her surroundings, fighting to maintain a balance between critique and endorsement, between rejection and complicity, between abstract thought and concrete action.

There are various levels where this balance or predicament—being torn between polar opposites that keep appealing to the artist—is played out in art theory, criticism, and history. For example, we examined the blurring of so-called high and low art as it was manifested by avant-garde artists in the twentieth century. One can recall Duchamp's *Fountain*, which in fact was an unmodified ("ready-made") urinal he displayed in a prestigious art exhibit under a pseudonym. Likewise, we can recall Warhol's depiction of Campbell's soup cans or Coca-Cola bottles, all in the name of breaking down the barriers of the "subject matter" appropriate for painting (bringing Berger's complaints of the elevated status of content and subject matter of Renaissance art within a contemporary context of discussion). The ideas associated with high and low art had to do, of course, with the ideals associated with high and low culture, with class stratification and economic positioning. The blurring of this distinction is also related to other common (and in our view mistaken) distinctions, such as pure versus commissioned art, between fine artists and commercial artists. Tracing the historical record of artworks, we were delighted to discover the paradox that while Renaissance artworks are perceived from our perspective as high and pure and fine, they were in fact commissioned pieces at the time (by popes and dukes, patrons and bourgeois merchants, who paid often on an hourly wage rate plus costs of materials, no different from paying other "laborers"). It is this paradox that reminds us of the economic and financial context within which the artistic community must operate (unless there are individual artists rich enough to eschew its trappings, and then, of course, they play right into the boundaries of these trappings).

The economic elements that influence how we produce art, namely, directly paying for someone to create a piece that we will eventually buy (or using a more elaborate mechanism of subsidizing art schools); how we distribute art, namely, using intermediaries, such as gallery owners and museum curators, art teachers and bureaucrats at endowment offices; and how we consume art in the sense of the cultural cues we follow from advertisement to fashion, from print media to photography and film. You don't need to study the history of economic systems in western civilization and their transformation over time in order to realize that whatever happens within a culture will be affected by such changes. You also don't need to be a marxist in order to realize that market-based economies with profit motives will operate differently from barter-based economies, for example. When art changes hands, then, does its value increase? Does it matter if a painting was bought or given as a gift? How do we even talk about the value of art?

For us, then, the approach to works of art is always already tainted, so to speak, by other social and economic cues (historically defined)—how much one paid for a piece, where it was acquired, what's the background of the artist, where the art is displayed. These elements or pieces of the value puzzle might be then reorganized in ideological terms, that is, bringing up political or ethical principles and ideals that inform the very framework in which we even ask questions about the value of art. Can art be valued for its own sake? Must we put a price tag next to a piece of art in order to value it properly? What legitimacy does one valuation have compared with another? By the time we begin to discuss legitimation, we come full circle to some of the issues we raised in the previous section about ideology as a set of beliefs and conviction one uses in order to legitimate a particular social order or practice. It's within this context that we also examined the public versus private art debates of the previous century, where the very notion of the privacy of any artwork was questioned. This set of concerns also grew out of a "leftist" critique of the confines of the elitist museum and gallery, where monetary tags separate socioeconomic classes and feed into the high/low art distinction. Those artists who wished to defy these distinctions or blur them were drawn to performance art and environmental installations, taking art to the streets and countryside as in previous generations when folk art and street fairs were open to any passerby.

Christo and Jeanne-Claude come to mind here not so much as artists who create works for outdoor viewing, and also find natural objects worthy of being "wrapped" and re-presented to the world under the guise of works of art, artifacts whose encounters with humanity render them worthy of an aesthetic experience. We push this theme in order to question the mindset, the intellectual backdrop against which such questioning takes place. It turns out that nineteenth-century ideals of "manifest destiny," for example, or those of the lone rider and the rugged individual who moved westward in northern America (for gold and glory), "conquering" or "discovering" the West (while annihilating Native Indians), have had an enormous influence over how we perceive our heritage and future. The promise of ultimate success in the "native" and "wild" and "primitive" landscape plays into the capitalist ideals of entrepreneurship (in terms of freedom to pursue one's "manifest destiny") so as to appeal to the American mind-set. But how does one portray this set of ideals, this ideology? Are the artists who visited the West prior to the Civil War, such as Bierstadt (landscapes) and Catlin (Indians), presenting the unlimited potential of the West "properly"? Is it nostalgia for a peaceful, heaven-like paradise to be inhabited here and now? Are they in fact painting commercials for the railroads and the new territories established there? Is there a more accurate or truthful depiction of the rough conditions under which the move to the West was undertaken? Should we perceive misery and pain, threats and dangers, starvation and conflict? Or rather be wowed to contemplate our own move to the western parts of the growing United States?

These rhetorical questions are of interest to us, since they in fact illustrate the extent to which artists and artworks became the visual carriers, the most powerful tools, of ideals and ideologies transmitted to the general public back East in the nineteenth century. The greatest orators of the day couldn't have had the same influence that one enormous painting, hung in a prominent place in New York or Philadelphia, had on visiting dignitaries as well as "common folk." Think of it as the television of today, a way to communicate and interact with thousands of people at once, and indirectly validate the idea of conquering the western territories. If you are a politician or military leader you can plead and threaten, cajole and bribe, but you always wish to appeal to one's heart and mind at once, make your pleas make sense right away, and have your audience "buy into" your vision. What better instrument of visualization than a painting or a photograph?

By the twentieth century enough revisionist historians had insisted that not everything in the past was good or fair or just, and that we must atone for our sins as an occupying, Eurocentrist, white male dominated culture. Painting a Native American, an American Indian, an indigenous American became itself a political statement of sorts, whether one attempted to glorify or pity. A young chief told us once, when we tried to introduce him "properly" that the proper designation meant nothing to him or his elders; "it doesn't matter what they call us," the elders said, "as long as they stop stealing our land." Once again, the terms and attitudes, the approach and behavior, personal and social, verbal and visual, end up embodying a political belief. So, when we discussed the works of the Christos we didn't limit ourselves to an aesthetic assessment or an examination of the financial arrangements they use in defiance of other methods of funding art projects, but also discussed the temporal and public nature of their works, where admission fee is not required, and where one's experience cannot become permanent (the Christos even own the photography rights to their works, not to mention their drawing and designs).

So, once again, though pretending to insist on the temporal nature of the aesthetic experience (Kant's and Burke's ahistorical notion of the sublime), there is a paradox in the Christos' control and record of their body of work, which is turned into a permanent "collection" or "exhibit" of sorts (one that easily lends itself to a "retrospective" show at a prestigious . . . museum, of course). The predicament never subsides, not even when the museum and gallery walls are thrust away in an attempt to break away from traditional viewing and the bourgeois trappings of the consumption of art. To focus on Christos' transcendence promise, then, is to ignore the inevitable contradiction they themselves and their artworks offer: an attempt to depoliticize that which is fully political (one can use the terms ideology and politics here interchangeably). This is an attempt to use the visual apparatus and its immediate public appeal to transcend the material conditions of human existence. By this we don't mean the classical (or romantic) desire for spiritual transcendence that is religious in nature and that pretends we can overcome our situation (even if the Christos themselves can be accused of this tendency). Rather, it's an attempt to realize, recognize, and internalize these same conditions and answer them not as if they are absent, but as if they are the obstacles that can never be overcome, and therefore require attention. The Christos, then, offer us a way of dealing with the inconsequential, yet monumental, role that artists play in the visualization of nature's beauty. Hence, they are purveyors and critics of our nostalgic view of that ideology of unadulterated, pristine beauty (see Illustrations 5a and 5b of the *Running Fence* being installed and its final display).

We also discussed in the earlier volume science and technology from two different perspectives. On the one hand, we suggested that avant-garde artists were quick to realize the potential of new techniques and materials, quick to experiment with new forms and styles, with new methods of mechanical and manual production and reproduction. On the other hand, from refined, nearly mechanical form of Brancusi's sculptures, we also learned to appreciate the aesthetic appeal of technological instruments, such as the propeller. Instead of simply thinking of technology as a way to perfect one's art and its expression, technical devices became themselves objects to admire for their beauty—can you say that a car is beautiful, that a bolt is? Artists, such as J. S. P. Boggs, went even further and turned our attention to the aesthetic value of money itself, the mode of exchange. Bills were copied and drawn, sold and used as having value similar to and exceeding the monetary denominations.

The avant-gardist approach to aesthetics, then, in this sense of reversing the gaze of the consumer, has been a useful illumination for us when embarking on our discussion of art, politics, and propaganda. It's less the psychological dimension that marketing wizards master that interest us, and more the ability to turn things around, to see the need for art in the dissemination of ideas and ideals, namely, politics and ideology. It's also the nature of the capitalist beast that in fetishizing our consumption, it pretends to depoliticize the economic conditions under which we live (see Buck-Morss 1995). By this we mean anything from the original "invisible hand" of Adam Smith (1776) to current depiction of the "free marketplace" where all are free to engage each other as equals (in Eagleton's sense). The marketplace is free and allows for equal competition only insofar as there is a legal framework to protect individual rights and claims, duties and responsibilities; and these political guidelines and guarantees are there if, and only if, there is a political platform that supports them. Once again we are back to ideology and politics, to promise and lies ("false consciousness," as Marxist critics call them) that determine (and not merely influence) how we live and interact within a society. When we are convinced that our destiny is in our hands, that we can change the conditions of our existence, and that we can transform ourselves into an ideal set up by others, then we have indeed bought into the ideology of the dominant class. The way this process of acceptance, subordination, and eventual motivated upward mobility works is through the medium of commercials and advertisement.

Berger hints at this, and we follow him and the avant-garde artists of the twentieth century all the way. For example, Jenny Holzer uses electronic signboards, such as the tower at Caesar's Palace in Las Vegas to flash messages from her "Truism Series" (see Illustration 6). These messages consist of one-line statements that assume conflicting points of views, such as "Save me from what I want." Her "fine art" advertising texts are shown to the public in a venue that typically displays announcements detailing the latest entertainment opportunities (Holzer 1977–1979, 24). No one stands there and tells us what to do; this would be un-American. No one tells us to maximize our credit card debt; this would be plain silly. Likewise, no one tells us that we have a chance to make it big, to become rich and famous and join the upper class. Yet, television networks advertise products and gadgets in such a way so as to convince the viewers that if we owned the product, we would indeed have "made it," joined the upper class, and become rich and famous. There are shows on television and colorful images in print media that illustrate the ways in which specific material possessions bring a smile to one's face, attract beautiful people to them, and ensure status and prestige otherwise unattainable. We don't exactly see Dürer's image of *Melancholy* advertised anywhere, nor Goya's depiction of Jeremiah. Why not? Perhaps the answer is that they are not "commercial-worthy visual materials" because they were not rich and famous, because they suffered for their ideas and prophecies, because they weren't "happy" (look at the colors, at their posture, at their thin figures). Consumerist culture in the twenty-first century still accepts the ideology of the Founding Fathers who promised in the Declaration of Independence the pursuit of happiness. Equality is left to old-fashioned Marxists, freedom is left to millionaires, and happiness is found in porn videos. What is left for the honest, hardworking citizen?

We should hasten to add, though, that unlike the Marxist critics, from Walter Benjamin and the Frankfurt School to more recent ones, such as Terry Eagleton and Stanley Aronowitz, we don't believe in a spiritual or emancipatory promise at the end of the rainbow. The dreadful role artists play in promoting political ideals is at times charming and fun, at times informative and critical, and at times manipulative and dangerous. Any American president who campaigns for election knows that, and is thus similar in his (so far) concerns to any old-fashioned (and some more contemporary) fascist leader, such as Mussolini and Stalin and Hitler. We are not claiming that they are similar in their ideology, of course. Yet we are claiming that they all need visual renderings to reach a wide audience, need to simplify their message, and vie for public appeal for their political agendas. Instead of focusing on politicians and ideologues, we focus on the torturous road on which artists find themselves when they ply their craft, as outsiders/insiders, profiteers, and dissidents.

III: THE ULTIMATE HOAX: THE ARTIST AS OUTSIDER

Artists in general, and avant-garde artists in particular, have been considered by some to have been the ultimate "outsiders" to the extent that their works are considered to be a critical assessment of political and cultural myths and icons. There is a sense in which a work of art is part of a discourse that responds to and critically engages that which preceded it. One can view the history of art as an ongoing conversation, wherein one generation has the opportunity to admire or undermine the works of those who preceded it. The canons of one era become the targets of the other. In retrospect, everything is open to revisions and reconsideration. One could imagine how this conversation is friendly in some cases and contentious in others; in some cases we expect a smooth continuation, and in the other a rift, a break, almost a rejection.

In the decade following Impressionism, the Pointillist style painters of Paris, for example, continued many of the concerns of their predecessors. They adopted the subject matter and color tonalities typical of Impressionistic style, while departing in the application of the paint as they reacted to the inherited tradition. However, in the post World War II United States, Abstract Expressionist artists emphatically rejected the Naturalist style and Social Realist subject matter of the American art that preceded them. They embraced abstract form and so-called sublime content in an attempt to underscore a completely radical shift from their immediate predecessors.

Now, it seems odd to appreciate the conversation in radical terms, because the very notion of being radical is problematic insofar as every individual is by definition a member of a community and is thereby influenced by the tradition into which he belongs, by default if not by design. But what happens if an artist is indeed a loner, an individual who refuses to conform or be part of any community whatsoever? Is this even possible? To some extent our answer is in the negative, because we can al-

WELCOME TO UCCS BOOKSTORE D64F06E06M06

        520 CASH-1   7352 0001 010

978014013515 NEW
BERGER/WAYS OF SEE   MDS 1   10.95
978073911261 NEW
SASSOWE/POLITICAL   MDS 1   24.95
              SUBTOTAL   35.90
   Sales Tax 7.4%   2.66
              TOTAL   38.56

ACCOUNT NUMBER XXXXXXXXXXXX7802 XX/XX
   Visa/Mastercard   38.56

Keep Receipt-Questions? 262-3247

                5/21/07   9:08 AM

* After Census date, as stated in UCCS schedule of courses, books are non-returnable.

New books must be in new selling condition, free from any marks or other signs of wear, and, if shrink-wrapped, the shrink-wrap must still be intact. All accessory items (CD, information cards etc.) originally included must also be returned undamaged.

GENERAL MERCHANDISE REFUNDS

Merchandise, General Books and Nursing Reference Books may be returned within 2 weeks (5 days for software and electronics) from the date of purchase and must be in original (new) condition.

1. Software must be in its original, sealed container.
2. Defective merchandise returned in (with) original packaging will be exchanged for the identical item.
3. All items on CLEARANCE are considered final sales and may not be returned
4. Computers carry the manufacturer's warranty.

SPECIAL ORDER ITEMS, STUDY AIDS, TEST PREPARATIONS, CLIFF NOTES, SPARK NOTES, BARCHARTS AND COMPUTER BOOKS ARE NON-RETURNABLE UNLESS DEFECTIVE AND THEN MAY BE EXCHANGED ONLY.

WHEN REFUNDS ARE AUTHORIZED, CASH WILL BE GIVEN FOR CASH/CHECK SALES AND THE ORIGINAL CREDIT CARD USED WILL BE CREDITED FOR CREDIT CARD SALES.

Klearimage.com

UCCS BOOKSTORE
PROTECT YOUR INVESTMENT
All refunds require the
original cash register receipt

TEXTBOOK REFUND DEADLINES
* Fall & Spring Semesters: 2 weeks from the date of purchase*

ways find, in a postmodernist or hermeneutical sense, a historical reference, a precedent, an antecedent. We should add here that there is a literal designation of Outsider Art that has currency within the vocabulary of art criticism. It refers to the creative work of individuals not trained in traditional institutions of art education, lacking apprenticeship experience with conventionally recognized artists, and therefore, presumably unaware of art history and tradition, styles and forms within canonical schools.

From a historical perspective, then, it's difficult to set oneself as an outsider. Yet, there are other senses in which the label outsider may make sense. One sense would be if the artistic community, rather than the canon of art history, excommunicated or set apart an artist from the rest of the establishment. For example, the avant-garde Surrealists, for example, officially rescinded Alberto Giacometti's membership in the group and excluded him from inclusion in the exhibition activities of the organization because of his exploration of subject matter not sanctioned by them nor conforming to surrealist methodology and ideology. The other sense is the casting aside, away, or imprisoning of artists by the political authorities for ideological reasons. For example, the geometric style of the Constructivists and Suprematist artists of the early Russian revolutionary period was banned by the Stalinist government when it declared Socialist Realism the official style of the state in 1926, an art of abstract form that was considered incapable of carrying the content and message of the Communist Party's ideology by its leaders. The Gestapo raided the Berlin Bauhaus Art School three months after Hitler became chancellor in 1933, arresting the faculty, confiscating the content in the premises, and as such eliminating one of its potential competitors for disseminating a vision of the future of an improved German society. We shall examine these two senses in turn. The consideration of what constituted a legitimate visual expression of the ideology of the revolution was not limited to government officials. The artistic community in the Soviet Union was intensely divided over the issue until the power of the state ended the debate over what style was appropriate for proletarian art (the art of the working class, similar to the science of the working class, in contra-distinction to bourgeois art and science).

But before we do so, we should note that our own brief musings about the notion of artists as outsiders are based on some sociological and anthropological studies on the topic. For example, there is a broad range of literature on foreigners as critics of the community in which they end up visiting or staying (Weber and de Tocqueville on America, or Durkheim on European transmigration). Similarly, the anthropologist who goes "native" so as not to contaminate the study with the prejudices of the outsider has been studied for generations (e.g., Margaret Mead and Ian Jarvie). There is also some discussion in the psychoanalytic world about schizophrenia as expressed linguistically (Laing and Laor), when different situations seem to be inside or outside the behavioral norms. All of these studies in effect remind us of the conventional wisdom of distinguishing between those within a tradition or canon, within the boundaries of a culture, who comprehend the cues of their visual environment, its syntax and semantics, and those outside the framework who just "don't get it."

The case of artists, in our view, differs little in theoretical terms from the cases described by anthropologists, linguists, and other critics. When artists are cast away from the establishment by political powers, there is a certain real quality about it, a practical dimension that in its pain exceeds theoretical confusions (just as the killing of a missionary is understood not merely as a religious conflict but a way to ward off uninvited intrusion and potential abuse). The reality of being outsiders was exemplified in the treatment of artists in the Soviet Union and Nazi Germany during periods of exile, purges, torture, and execution. Typically, whatever survived persecution and destruction by the authorities has been posthumously sanctified in terms of critical subversion and courage. One striking example of post World War II has been the German Expressionist Max Beckmann, whose work was among the art condemned by Hitler as being "degenerate" and now sells for millions in auction houses, such as Sotheby's and Christie's.

But the painful reality of being outsiders has been adopted wholeheartedly by many artists who wish to turn this painful reality into a selling myth. What is at stake here, then, is the ability to distinguish one's work from that of all the others because it is cast as if it were outside the norm, exceptional in terms of its message. In short, this is the typical view of the avant-garde attempt to distance themselves from the rest of their community. Part of what is evoked here is the myth of the lonely, creative genius fighting a stodgy, sleepy, overbearing artistic establishment that is incapable of understanding the latest twists in artistic progress.

Without questioning the reality of pain and suffering of many twentieth-century artists who were targeted by dictators and oppressive regimes around the world, we wish to suggest the very notion of "outsider" is problematic in general, and has specific connotations when it gets to artworks. All artworks are part of a canon, even if they are not included in standard educational texts or national propaganda. We say this because we believe that the production, distribution, and consumption of any piece of art are part of a cultural and economic discourse and reality. This discourse and practice is suggestive and informative even when it jettisons some artworks for a while, only to rediscover and lionize those years later. For example, the Musee d'Orsay now prominently displays many nineteenth-century sculptures and paintings in the Salon or Academic style that were never given exhibition space for most of the twentieth century in any credible museum of fine art because they failed to adhere to the criteria of the established canon of the day.

With the elasticity portrayed by late capitalism, a way to include any form of production, distribution, and consumption even when it seems to allegedly contradict the conditions of capitalism, artworks and the artistic community have been able to accommodate any and all forms of expression. Before you know it, Folk Art is being displayed in museums, television shows are judged on their artistic merits, and the National Endowment for the Arts is subsidizing performance art. Almost all critical objections are brought into the artistic fold with proper funding and media hype. The matrix of the art world expands so as to accommodate, even if not fully endorse, all that is out there, offering to commodify, label, and price appropriately every piece of art.

In this sense, then, artists are insiders even when they deliberately insist on being outsiders. Their artworks, in two-dimensional mediums, music, dance, and other areas of performance, find an audience even when that audience refuses to engage in the regular exchange process of money for entertainment. In addition to gallery openings and multinational art exhibits, there are street musicians who participate in newly formed street fairs and festivals, where mimes and acrobats, posters and T-shirt images, have become an integral part of the artistic community and the aesthetic experience. Whether we label this Folk Art or Dissident Art, it is still art that is consumed (in the sense of being paid for by someone, being sold and bought for a price). The integrated promotion of high and low art—from museum shops to postcards and advertisements—has been a clever move to include all art forms as part of capitalist enjoyment. Is there anything we cannot buy or sell, distribute and consume? Whenever a willing buyer (what was thought of previously or traditionally as an audience) is found, the artistic endeavor and experience are engaged, and artists are as much insiders as outsiders, even when they remain street vendors or garret monks. Now we should note that the elitist "buyer" could be someone merely watching a performance at a street fair, presumably not paying for the performance, yet still buying a hot dog or soda and thereby buying into the context, framework, and ideology of the marketplace, where everything is for sale. In some cases, the vendors pay a fee to the city that may subsidize the (free) performance, so that the hot-dog buyer indirectly pays for the performance, after all.

IV: THE IDEOLOGY OF ART, THE ART OF IDEOLOGY

As we continue to examine the politics of the artistic context, we plan to examine the lessons artists learned in the twentieth century in regard to the political context in which they had to work, so as to appreciate their predicament in the present century. More specifically, we contend that there were two parallel paths undertaken by artists in the Western world. One path was perceived to be dictated by political power relations and interest, as can be observed with the behavior of Soviet artists after the Bolshevik revolution, German artists during the Nazi Reich, and even American artists during the two world wars. In the two cases one can find a similarity in the ways in which national interests occupied the content and the style of artistic works to the extent that it is possible to detect a "national" style and even national icons. We should hasten to add that our brief survey is not meant to have a strong moral component to it, but is rather used so as to ascertain whether it is possible to speak of artworks in national or political terms. We should also hasten to remind ourselves here that to claim a political label is problematic. Obviously, everything is political: the choice of what artistic medium to enjoy—an opera versus a rock concert, a museum versus graffiti. Yet, if everything is political, then there is nothing special or significant in this designation. So instead of trivializing this designation, we'd like to bolster its meaning in the context of appreciating the special, even crucial, role artworks play in the political arena.

Back to the different paths. The other path was perceived to be influenced (if not dictated) by technoscientific developments of the past century. These developments set the stage for the use of new mediums, new styles, and even new audiences. From the confines of the gallery and the museum, artworks were displayed in nature, so to speak, as in the case of the Christos, or were communicated electronically through television and the Internet, or in the case of Jenny Holzer's art, electric billboards. Unlike the other path, in this one there is a tendency toward universality and global imagery, so that the language of art is interpreted and understood internationally.

Our delineation of these two developmental paths in the past century is meant only as a convenient tool with which to ask the following question: Is it possible to do art for art's sake? Is it possible to avoid any and all political influences and escape the pressure of power structures? Or, have the Soviet and Nazi artists been more genuine in their acceptance of their own obedience to the dominant power elite that enforced its cultural symbols, icons, and message?

The last question might sound perverse and counterintuitive, but it is not. The predicament of artists has been and will always remain their own complicity in the affairs of the state while maintaining a critical attitude as well. What we have called elsewhere (Sassower and Cicotello, 2000) their detached attachment is a balancing act that can be condemned as politically naïve if not an outright sellout. Furthermore, the politics of the state at times pales by comparison to the influence of the politics of the artistic community. For example, are the museum curator and the gallery owner not as terrifying with their capricious choices and preferences as political leaders and party functionaries? Are art collectors not as overbearing and authoritative as propaganda ministers of yesteryears? Don't they wield their authoritative judgment as if there are no alternatives, as if "the truth of the matter" is transparent, and obedience by others is mandated?

Perhaps we tend to be more forgiving toward the choices artists make when faced with their predicament because we believe that the technoscientific world (from tools to telecommunication) is itself political. It is political in terms of power relations within sovereign states, the dominance of money over cultural productions, and the concentration of economic and political power in the hands of the few. So, the very pretense of artistic (cultural) neutrality and purity evaporates before our eyes. Perhaps the next question should be: If purity is an artistic impossibility, can authenticity save the souls of artists? And if the answer is yes, do we mean by authenticity so-called Folk Art, or the integrity of individual artists?

1

2

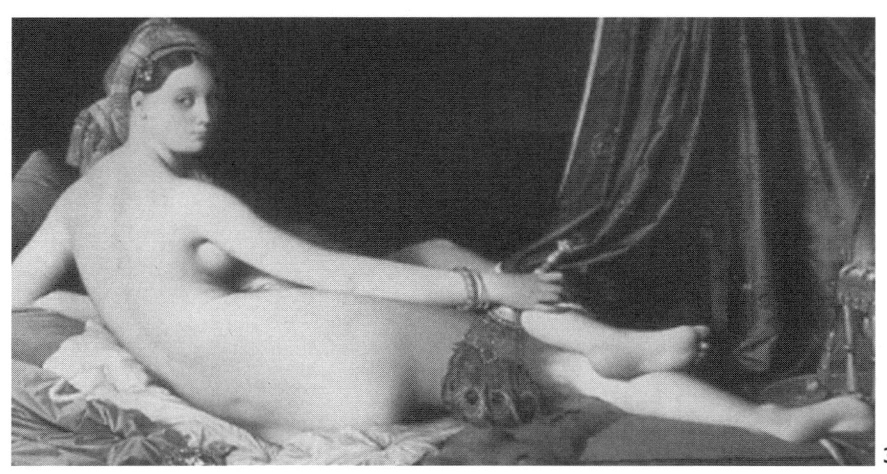

3

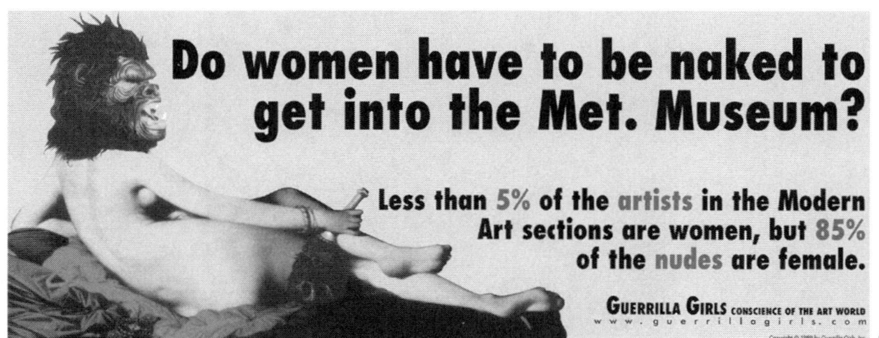

Do women have to be naked to get into the Met. Museum?
Less than 5% of the artists in the Modern Art sections are women, but 85% of the nudes are female.
GUERRILLA GIRLS CONSCIENCE OF THE ART WORLD
www.guerrillagirls.com
Copyright © 1989 by Guerrilla Girls, Inc.

4

5a

5b

CAESARS
PALACE
PROTECT ME
FROM WHAT
I WANT
TEXACO
PARKING
Denny's

6

2

THE VISUAL FRAMING OF
FASCISM AND DEMOCRACY

I: IDEOLOGY AS MYTH-MAKING

As we explained in the previous chapter, in order to express ideas and disseminate them to a wide audience, politicians and political parties employ the visual messages of artists. Whether understood in terms of Stalin's Soviet Union, Mussolini's Italy, or Hitler's Germany, what fascism, for example, has relied on for its popular appeal was a strong propaganda machine that in turn relied on images and icons that were produced by artists (some volunteered, some were coerced). Instead of arguing about the aesthetic merits of these artworks or about the moral principles that might be violated under these conditions, we are interested in examining the process by which these images are "read." It is obvious that the ideas that constitute an ideology can be and usually are expressed pictorially. But what is less obvious, but more informative from our perspective, is the fact that these ideas are read backwards by viewers.

The image is often the first encounter we have with an idea, and only then an interpretive process leads us to its origins, so to speak, its foundations. Hence the predicament of ideological dissemination: Have the ideas been read properly? Have the right ideas come across with the right message? In the process of leading the viewer through a maze of interpretation, political parties feel the need to control every aspect and every movement of the potential or targeted viewer. In doing so, they inadvertently admit that the image is so powerful on its own that it may not reflect accurately the subtleties of the ideas behind it or that it may even unwittingly subvert these ideas. For example, is the *Statute of Liberty* a symbol of freedom and hope for ideological export, or an invitation for generations of immigrants coming to our shores? How do our current immigration policies square with the symbol and with the ideology that gave rise to it or that has to catch up with its more recent interpretations?

It is, then, also in this respect that we examine here works of art in the service of ideology to evaluate if they are in fact representing a specific national character, their identification as being American, German, Italian, Soviet, and the like. Just as there is a national pressure under fascism to see the world in particular ways and to see one's fellow citizens as having specific roles to play in that world (whether seen as collaborators within the state or liberators when confronting other states, spreading the "word" of their leaders as the gospels are spread by missionaries), there is a similar ideological zeal under democracy to share one's ideological convictions. These processes will be examined here as they pertain to what one could call an "essentialist" view of imagery and identity, namely, the view that an image represents precisely the ideas that give rise to its creation, while we leave the question of a universal appeal versus national identity to the next chapter.

In this chapter, then, we begin with an examination of the link between ideology and myth-making in contemporary culture; then examine the Russian and Mexican revolutions of the past century so as to see the ways in which artistic renditions were used in both cases respectively to validate political aspirations and social objectives; and, finally, we move to the four parallel trends in American art of that period so as to illustrate the pressure under which artists are regularly put: the military (war effort), labor organization (unions), advertisement for products, and the pastoral West, all in the name of democracy. We'd like to show how similar the artistic faces of democracy are to those of fascism when it comes to images and the ideological messages sent through these images (such as, heroism, wholesomeness, and hope). This way, we'd be in a better position to understand if indeed there is a universal language of art or a national visual code discernable only with preset national boundaries.

Myths play an important role in supporting ideologies and perpetuating a cultural identity. They are, so to speak, the foundations on which ideological claims are made. Though seemingly fictional in nature, something that is untrue, almost a lie we tell about ourselves, about others, or about a situation we describe to someone who doesn't know better, myths have been understood by anthropologists and others as stories we tell in order to make sense of our past and our present. Myths can interpret or present a story or narrative that in its presentation makes sense of a set of beliefs, rituals, or ceremonies that otherwise would seem incoherent, if not outright silly. Not that we wish to delve too deeply into this topic, but we appreciate the similarities between those studying the images of myths as ways through which to read retrospectively, so to speak, the actual myths and the stories they tell. Likewise, if we can study myths and their images at all, are we not indeed admitting that there is a common, if not uniform or universal, story line that can be traced in all of them? Is it the content, the form, or the style that renders them objects of study to begin with?

Now myths can be about gods and supernatural beings, about natural phenomena that might not lend themselves readily to a rational explanation, or about the origins of human existence (whether we read the ancient Greeks or the Bible). There are long traditions of myth interpretation, when scholars attempt to uncover layers of meaning not easily revealed on first reading (or hearing) a myth. There are anthropologists, such as Claude Levi-Strauss, who focus on linguistic elements and structures, on repetitive and cross-cultural cues that could transcend the specificity of one tribe or one myth. There are psychologists, such as Carl Jung and Sigmund Freud, who find dream sequences worthy of analysis for both the cultural baggage (archetypes) and personal impact (of the collective unconscious) they have on us.

Myths, then, are important to study if one wishes to understand the background and the present conditions of a society. Myths can help bring a group of individuals together, and keep them so. They provide symbolic features that can be perceived in a culture or emulated, if the culture needs to redefine itself or find its core beliefs and foundations. The metaphors myths encompass, as Ernest Cassier suggests, can be read and decoded, so as to better align particular communal behaviors with what is claimed on their behalf. There are great popularizers, such as Joseph Campbell, who endeared distant people and foreign cultures to Western minds by illustrating the extent to which myths can be the single most significant instrument by which to delve into the innermost psyche of ancient people and current groups, finding features that are similar and different, features that can be immediately grasped because of their visual and spiritual power. Of course, one can see in myths the nascent ingredients that eventually we recognize as "science" and scientific thought, as Frazer and Malinowski argue. This means, in short, that myths bring order to chaos, set up functional structures one can appreciate for their simplicity and their explicit way of bringing together natural variables that would otherwise remain obscure, impenetrable, or magical. The rational basis of myth-making or myth interpretation allows us to read retrospectively that which wasn't as clear at the time. Myths, in this respect, are constructed and repeated in order to make sense; commonsense appeals to any rational human being, however "primitive"; and logic as we know it today is nothing but an extension of common sense.

The ritualistic and ceremonial components of myths are less interesting to us here, for they remain in the domain of religious scholars and those interested in certain sacred and spiritual promises myths provide. For us, myths are tools by which a phenomenon is explained. Let's just recall briefly the myth of origins as the Bible presents it in contradistinction to the Greeks. Here is one brief paraphrasing: God created Adam in His own image; Adam was lonely and complained to God; when he fell asleep, God took one of his ribs and created Eve. And the rest is history . . . Here is another: Zeus created three kinds of people, male, females, and a mixture of the two, each of whom have two heads, four hands, and four legs. Since these creatures moved fast and became arrogant, Zeus punished them by cutting them in half. Hence, we keep on looking for our other half . . .

Obviously, in our culture the first myth sounds more "real" than the other; it "makes sense." But what does it make sense of? Perhaps it simply provides a textual reference point to what we have heard over the years—there is a sacred text, the Bible, we can read. Perhaps it tells us that the only "natural" or "divine" union is the one between a male and female. Perhaps it reminds us that in order to perpetuate the human race, we need a heterosexual couple to procreate or multiply, as Abraham was instructed by God. Who knows? It might be sanctioning our social and moral codes, setting the tone of what ought to be the case.

But let's ponder, for a minute, the Greek variant of the myth of human origins. On some level, it's no more nor less incredible that Zeus cut humans into two than that God created a female out of Adam's rib. These supernatural powers are meant to remind us of what we must do, how we should behave, and what we should avoid. The Greeks tell us that in fact heterosexual attraction accounts for only a third of the human race, while homosexual and lesbian coupling is the majority. Moreover, the cliché of "finding one's other or better half" is equally applicable to hetero- and homosexual relationship. That is, homosexuality is just as "natural" and "divine" as its alternative. This might seem as a small point, but it speaks to the cultural biases and prejudices into which we buy or which we reject when encountering these myths as explanatory and justifying tools. Take any election in the United States, and you'd be more likely to encounter a politician citing the Bible as the basis for opposing gay marriage than someone citing Plato's *Symposium*. Is it because we are not Greek enough? Or is it because Socrates was not divinely inspired, as Moses and Jesus were? Well, Socrates appealed to the oracle of Delphi for his inspiration. But it was a female oracle, after all . . .

We should note that the terms legend and folktale are sometimes used interchangeably with myth, and that perhaps the "sacred" element of myths gives them additional authority, one to which politicians are inclined to appeal. As Donna Rosenberg explains,

> A myth is a *sacred* story from the past. It may explain the origin of the universe and of life, or it may express its culture's moral values in human terms. Myths concern the powers that control the human worlds and the relationship between those powers and human beings . . . A folktale is a story that, in its plot, is pure fiction and that has no particular location in either time or space. However, despite its elements of fantasy, a folktale is actually a symbolic way of presenting the different means by which human beings cope with the world in which they live . . . A legend is a story from the past about a subject that was, or is believed to have been, historical. (Rosenberg 1994)

We aren't sure that these distinctions are useful, as we have seen the Greek way of suggesting, and explaining, and referring back to their legends, their folktales, and their myths. When articulated to an audience, whatever is conveyed is not labeled as such, and there is ample opportunity to hear whatever you want in whatever manner you want to hear it. Regardless of how one defines myths, most cultures find them useful as ways of holding their "truths" together. Moreover, as Susan Josephson agrees, myths also function as a way to place us in the world—at the center, if we follow the Adam and Eve story—so that we have a moral sense of our role in nature in relation to other animals and the environment (Josephson 1996, 191–4). The extension, for example, of the Biblical image of creation leads "naturally" to the nuclear family, where images of wholesome mother and father, staring at each other lovingly, hold one or more children in their laps, young and healthy and pretty. Illustration 7 is a typical Norman Rockwell "Americana scene" image: *The Freedom from Want* a.k.a. *The Thanksgiving Dinner* of 1943. The "ideal" traditional family unit celebrating a national holiday is a theme that has similar depictions in the poster images of Nazi, Italian Facist, and Soviet ideologies.

Throughout history, artists have been inspired by myths to give them visual form, to set humanity in its proper place, so to speak. If one were to suggest that biblical stories are myths in the senses delineated above, then one can find a rich history of artworks that were commissioned by the Catholic Church and many of its wealthy followers over the centuries to depict these stories and remind the audiences of what God expects of them. In fact, we tell our students that they ought to read the Bible if they want to appreciate the references, the subject matter, and the moral of the stories that are readily portrayed in history books and in art museums. To some extent, our less Biblically educated students read backward from artworks to the Bible, seeing these works as remnants of a culture and its belief system (which might be more accurate for cultures committed to oral rather than textual history).

The anthropologist James Clifford sets the stage of modern ethnographic studies, themselves limited to reading backwards from oral history, archeological digs, or remains of used objects, as a viewing of images and ideas retrospectively. But what is it that we "read" or observe? We have artifacts, objects of art, and other items that either have been already collected or that we begin to collect in order to understand a culture other than our own. Just as we think that anyone who watches American television shows can learn about our ideas and our culture, so we believe that we can uncover the mysteries of other cultures by observing their material foot tracks. For him, then, the "classic analysis of Western 'possessive individualism'" (of Macpherson in 1962), is a reminder of the capitalist setting where value and self-identity were (and still are) rooted in and depended on the ownership of material objects (Clifford 1988, 217).

This sense of self and one's position within a culture was an ideal, a way to translate an ideology into personal terms. The ideology of advanced capitalism valued wealth in material terms and therefore could easily induce individualism to perceive this expression of wealth in terms of personal ownership, private property. This way of being was rationalized and institutionalized so that the individual was at the center of attention surrounded by a set of artifacts acknowledged to be valued and validated by the culture as a whole. In his words:

> A history of anthropology and modern art needs to see in collecting both a form of Western subjectivity and a changing set of powerful institutional practices . . . What criteria validate an authentic culture or artistic product? What are the differential values placed on old and new creations? What moral and political criteria justify "good," responsible, systematic collecting practices? (Ibid., 221)

Clifford echoes here some of the points made by Berger in regard to oil paintings of the Renaissance as objectifying and reifying a set of material possessions that are privileged and framed, owned and displayed by the bourgeoisie. Likewise, he echoes the concerns of art historians, such as Michele Bogart, who appreciate the extent to which commercial conditions of the twentieth century have influenced the practices of all artists, whether they wish to call themselves "fine" or "commercial" artists, whether they work for themselves, so to speak, or for an advertising agency.

When Clifford explains the ways in which we observe retrospectively works of art and insist that what has been collected from a specific time period or a region is indicative of the time and place and provides an excellent way of reading back in time about the ideological commitments and cultural practices of a group of people, we might be insisting too much and with a wrong emphasis. For him, the very mechanism that legitimates and privileges one practice or set of symbols and artifacts over another is also open to set in motion changes:

> While the object systems of art and anthropology are institutionalized and powerful, they are not immutable. The categories of the beautiful,

the cultural, and the authentic have changed and are changing. Thus it is important to resist the tendency of collections to be self-sufficient, to suppress their own historical, economic, and political processes of production. (Ibid., 229)

It seems to us that Clifford the anthropologist has much to say about the work of art historians who routinely cast a set of artworks as if they have gained over time a status beyond reproach, a framework that cannot be revised. This is true of those talking about ancient Egyptian artifacts as well as Renaissance paintings. Of course these designations are convenient tools with which to approach a period or a set of works, but let's remember that convenience in itself doesn't legitimate or cast in stone categories and classifications. Convenient shortcuts in life can be misleading and dangerous, pretending that something is the case when in fact it's not. Here is an interesting example, relating to the political upheaval about billboard posters in New York at the beginning of the last century.

As Michele Bogart tells the story, what began as simply a colorful, and aesthetically pleasing advertising, turned into a "social evil." The forces that wanted to limit and even abolish billboards claimed that "aesthetic considerations were as legitimate a basis for social regulations as are sanitary conditions," while those who wished to maintain the right to advertise anywhere were supported by the legal system that claimed that "aesthetics were a matter of luxury and indulgence rather than of necessity, and it is necessity alone which justifies the exercise of police power" (Bogart 1995, 97). At the end of the day, competing ideologies found their way into the legal system, itself a by-product of the mythmaking American ideology (of the inalienable rights to private property, for example, and the freedom to express publicly one's personal tastes and preferences), and the commitment to private property overrode any and all other social and aesthetic considerations. Here, too, anthropologists who might be studying the development of commerce in New York one hundred years ago should be careful to consider not only artifacts (posters and photographs of them), but also the legal battle that raged when they were displayed. This would enrich the study and ensure that it wouldn't be too skewed in the direction of uninhibited endorsement of capitalist modes of distribution and consumption.

So, the myth of American capitalism as the forward march from poverty to prosperity, from misery to happiness, could be self-serving for some and quite devastating for others. It's not necessarily that myth-making is exclusively in the hands of the powerful and "ruling classes" in some sense of the term, or that it's necessarily undertaken in bad faith, but it seems to portray a picture of our life that might be partial, incomplete, or simply false. (See Illustration 8 of John Gast's *American Progress* of 1883; it is an image of the myth of Manifest Destiny as the ideology of conquest of the western American frontier). Note here that Terry Eagleton doesn't equate all ideological pronouncements as necessarily "false" in any sense of the term, because in many cases, he suggests, "it is quite possible for a ruling order to make pronouncements which are ideological in the sense of buttressing its own power, but which are in no sense false" (Eagleton 1991, 26). So, it could be fairly argued that indeed progress is at hand, it just depends how one measures it. Do we focus on the shift of white, male life expectancy in the United States from 47 in 1900 to 74 in 2000? Or do we focus on the shrinking of the "middle class" by the end of the twentieth century, as the rich have gotten richer and the poor poorer?

At this juncture, it might be useful to recall Eagleton's forebearers in this arena, namely, the neo-Marxists of the Frankfurt School. When Max Horkheimer and Theodor Adorno approached the art world as a community of artists enmeshed in capitalist production, they had no problem calling their activities "The Culture Industry." As much as we can tell, this is a less lofty designation of culture in the sociological or anthropological terms, and more closely aligned with economic conditions and financial rewards. They begin by suggesting that "culture today is infecting everything with sameness." This declaration must come as a surprise to those who'd have us think that culture is indeed an antidote to the technoscientific world in which the twentieth century found itself. In this sense, then, capitalist production, distribution, and consumption, based as it is on the marketplace, plays into the hands of and supports technoscientific developments.

For Horkheimer and Adorno there is something perverse about this process that permeates every element in our culture and our life; the one doesn't provide reprieve from the other. As they claim: "In reality, a cycle of manipulation and retroactive need is unifying the system ever more tightly." For them, "technical rationality," is promoted by those with economic interests to benefit from its increasing prevalence, and therefore they call it "the rationality of dominance" (Horkheimer and Adorno 2002, 95). They use the term rationality in order to underscore both the structure of the system and its hold on its participants. This kind of dominance seems almost inevitable; because it's rational and not capricious, it makes sense rather than seems bizarre. In short, it's welcomed rather than rejected. As such, this kind of dominance is no dominance at all! If those with economic interests can acquire their benefits in a manner that seems reasonable to those from whom they are benefiting, and if they can sell their ideology without compromise or remorse, then they have become able communicators and keen observers of human nature and its needs.

As we understand this, myth-making and ideology have less to do with a story of origins or of divine order, but are tools in the hands of those who'd like capitalist modes of exchange to be the only means according to which humans act, react, and interact. According to this view (by contrast to, say, the communist myths still operational in China), there is no pretense that there is anything but capitalism in this modern world, understood as a self-interested and voluntary exchange of goods and services; there is no pretense that there are any loftier goals than those enumerated by capitalist ideology, at least in the sense of optimizing one's profits from an exchange and accumulating wealth. And if this ideology needs any justification or legitimation, if it indeed needs any ideals and principles as a foundation, then we can always remind everyone of freedom and equality, individual prosperity and happiness. This is true for those who live the capitalist dream (or nightmare) and those who hear about it. Now, of course, freedom and equality are vague terms that have undergone some transformation over the years: we speak of circumscribed freedom and equal opportunity. This way, we acknowledge the constraints on one's freedom in terms of the freedom of others, and we admit that there is no absolute equality (since humans are always different from each other in natural talents and propensities), but instead we compromise with equal opportunity, the promise that anyone can pursue the American dream.

But the American dream, for one, is not a set of ideas and principles people remember and to which they adhere. Instead, it's a set of images they come across daily when they watch television at home and when they travel to work. Billboards and advertising are splashed across any surface that is visible to the eye, and it's there that the American dream finds its expression and resting point. But are these images critical or even self-critical? Do they admit to being self-serving for those who paid for them? Or do they, by contrast, pretend to be merely stating the obvious, bringing together the ideas and ideals we have always believed in and for which we fight wars? When Horkheimer and Adorno respond in the negative to all of these rhetorical questions, they remind us that the power of art, in a political sense, is to assume its absolute nature, its steadfast foundation as if truth and stability, honesty and integrity, have always accompanied works of art. In their words: "By claiming to anticipate fulfillment through their aesthetic derivatives, it posits the real forms of the existing order as absolute. To this extent the claims of art are always also ideology." But this doesn't mean that artworks don't have the potential to be critical and self-critical, betray change and transformation, promise hope and revolution.

As they continue: "Yet it is only in its struggle with tradition, a struggle precipitated in style, that art can find expression for suffering. The moment in the work of art by which it transcends reality cannot, indeed, be served from style; that moment, however, does not consist in achieved harmony, in the questionable unity of form and content, inner and outer, individual and society, but in those traits in which the discrepancy emerges, in the necessary failure of the passionate striving for identity." But does art, do artists, and do those who sponsor them push artworks in that direction of "failure," that is, in the direction that admits to moments of transcendence beyond the dominance of the capitalist culture industry? No, they say: "Instead of exposing itself to this failure, in which the style of the great work of art has always negated itself, the inferior work has relied on its similarity to others, the surrogate of identity. The culture industry has finally posited this imitation as absolute" (Ibid., 103).

By understanding culture as an industrialized and "rigorously subsumed" element of the whole, do Horkheimer and Adorno explain the industry of culture or the culture of industry? Do they politicize the aesthetic domain or do they add an aesthetic dimension to the political and ideological framework that protects and perpetuates capitalism? We believe that they do both, but in order to accomplish their critical analysis, they demonstrate how these domains are intertwined. To emphasize the extent to which there is no escape from the clutches of capitalist industrialization, they conclude:

> Only by subordinating all branches of intellectual production equally to the single purpose of imposing on the senses of human beings, from the time they leave the factory in the evening to the time they clock on in the morning, the imprint of the work routine which they must sustain throughout the day, does this culture mockingly fulfill the notion of a unified culture which the philosophers of the individual personality held out against mass culture. (Ibid., 104)

"Mass culture," or what later in the century has been called in America "Popular Culture," is unified in a frightening way, because it allows no refuge for "individual personality." The paradox of capitalism, then, is that in order to focus on the individual and the rights associated with her or his activities, the dominant forces of the economy have erased her or him. Yes, we still promote the ideology of individualism, but we don't want the reality to be apparent (or even exist). For if the individual were to become too forceful, submission would not be possible; if individual tastes were to become pervasive, how could mass production satisfy diverse tastes and preferences? How do you mass market a mass-produced commodity to individuals who assert their differences? Even "individualism" is marketed with aftermarket accessories that are supposed to express individual departures from the mass-marketing of the original product. Individualism, then, is circumscribed by available mass-marketed accessories. Other personal or individual expressions that deviate too much from the mainstream "aftermarket" scheme turn out to be seen as eccentric because they fail to conform to the norms of the prefigured, appropriate deviant choices. These questions are being studied and answered by marketing gurus today. They, too, would agree that we must return to the study of human nature and the psychosocial dynamics of advanced capitalism in order to figure out the next steps that the capitalist enterprise must take. And when the return to basic ideas—the ideology of guiding myths—is initiated, we come back to Horkheimer and Adorno's observations about the tendency to "buy into" an ideology:

> . . . just as the ruled have always taken the morality dispensed to them by the rulers more seriously than the rulers themselves, the defrauded masses today cling to the myth of success still more ardently than the successful. They, too, have their aspirations. They insist unwaveringly on the ideology by which they are enslaved. (Ibid., 106)

Myth-making, then, is not a pasttime of the "rulers" or the dominant class, but an active program to ensure the continuity of the capitalist system. The program is effective when "the only escape from the work process in factory and office is through adaptation to it in leisure time" (Ibid., 109). Leisure time itself is subsumed in the work process, in the monetary demands it exacts of those wishing to forget their work. And the aesthetic elements that make leisure time different from the workplace are themselves constructed by a workplace and consumed within a different workplace, but a workplace nonetheless.

Terry Eagleton agrees with the Frankfurt School's critique of the collapse of art into the capitalist and technoscientific culture in which it finds expression, and so he posits:

> if art is subject like everything else to the law of objectification, it cannot avoid a kind of fetishism. . . . Art's autonomy is a form of reification, reproducing what it resists; there can be no critique without the objectification of spirit, but critique thus lapses to the status of thinghood and so threatens to undo itself. The modernist culture Adorno espouses cannot help positing itself as independent of any conditions of material production, and so insidiously perpetuates false consciousness; but the fetishistic character of the work is also a condition of its truth, since it is its blindness to the material world of which it is a part which enables it to break the spell of the reality principles. (Eagleton 1991, 351–2)

Myth-making and ideology, ideas and principles, are useful tools with which to control people and remind them of their place in the natural order and the roles they must play. If benign, then it's a helpful tool with which to reassure anxious people of the meaning of their life; if dangerous, then it's a manipulative tool with which to exact fear and submission, or at least a way to mobilize for whatever cause is being promoted (war, revolution, changes in lifestyle choices). Art can be found in either case. But can the analysis of artworks and the artists who produce them give us a hint as to which case it is? Can we see through the images the underlying messages and intent of their patrons and sponsors? These questions will occupy us in the next section.

II: REVOLUTIONARY PROMISES: THE SOVIET UNION AND MEXICO

However different the conditions of Russia and Mexico in the beginning of the past century were, they brought about political changes that were cast in ideological terms, and succeeded in their respective ways with the aid of the industry of artists. We don't pretend to give here a historical analysis or a philosophical backdrop to events that surrounded and culminated, for example, in the October Revolution or in the work of Trotsky on Mexico. Rather, we'd like to illustrate, as briefly as possible, how certain artistic movements and styles conformed or were rejected because they did or didn't convey the proper messages as understood by political leaders. The purpose of this section is to review the struggles and misunderstandings of the Soviet Constructivists on the one hand and Diego Rivera on the other. Of course there are cultural and indigenous differences across the continents, but we would like to tease out some of the similarities.

We need not rehearse in detail the Marxist (read socialist and communist) ideals that informed the overthrow of the feudal system of Russia under the Tsars. The notions of freedom for all citizens and equality among all workers were some of the ideals that the Communist Party worked with. The nuances of the debates that culminated in the revolution and the rise to power of Lenin's version of Statism (state-controlled socialism rather than a more humanistic variant) does not concern us here. Nor are we concerned with the details of the programs by which a feudal, agrarian system was replaced by an industrial, urban system of production. Likewise, the Five-Year Plans that were enacted with emphasis on social goods and services rather than consumer goods is unimportant here. But what is important is the artistic means by which the Party imparted its ideals and their implementation.

These images were informed by the "workers of the world unite" ideal, for example, and as such required a whole different visual vocabulary that differed from church iconography or aristocratic refinements of the traditional European sort. The "Reds" of the new government promised to include the participation of all citizens, particularly the previously disenfranchised workers and peasants. One could read into the very color red a sense of passion and commitment, a matter of emotional appeal to the hearts of the workers rather than their minds alone (a refrain no different from Rousseau's insistence that the Enlightenment may have made us more learned, but much less moral than we were when in the State of Nature). The red flags and symbols added the hammer and the sickle in the strong hands of workers, reminding the new soviets and communes of the basic need for agriculture and industry.

The Constitution of the Russian Socialist Federal Soviet Republic adopted in July 1918 clearly declares its fundamental aim to be the "abolition of all exploitation of man by man, the complete elimination of the division of society into classes, the ruthless suppression of the exploiters, the establishment of a socialist organization of society and the victory of socialism in all countries" (White 1988, 18). If the new regime were to carry out the kind of radical transformation of the old monarchy and aristocracy into a classless society where each citizen would contribute to the whole according to her or his abilities, and each would receive in return from the whole according to her or his needs (rather than maintain an exploitive process where the poor slaved away for the rich and made them richer), then a cultural revolution needed to be carried out as well. Lenin understood this fact, and set about to commission visual forms of communication that would speak to every citizen and would be understood by all. An important reason for this was the lack of a literate proletariat outside of the major urban areas. The census of 1920 would reveal only 45 percent literacy in the territories controlled by the Soviet government.

The pressing need to solidify the new government's control in the immediate postrevolutionary civil war period made it even more crucial that effective visual images and programs would be in place. Having a sprawling country with a largely rural and illiterate people, and having to break down traditional modes of communication (between landlords and their serfs, for example, or between the Orthodox Church's priests and their parishioners) with their iconography, instilled a sense of urgency for the new regime. Winning the hearts and minds of the people, while still fighting the old regime, the entrenched opposition of the

"Whites," was just as difficult as winning the hearts and minds of those within the artistic community. Old habits and customs of patronage found new outlets for those resisting the revolution in the use of posters; many well-established and sophisticated artists of the prerevolutionary period aligned themselves with the old regime, expecting the upheavals of the day to subside. The Reds figured out that they had to play the same game, use the same medium used so effectively by the Whites. And indeed, as an official in charge of distributing posters for the Whites admitted, "the Bolshevik posters had been more powerful than cannon or bullets" in the struggle for their cause (Ibid., 115). The battlefield shifted, so to speak, from the ground to the air, from the rolling hills to the bulletin boards.

Because poster art became the primary vehicle for the communication of ideology, officials were not just content to use the traditional static surfaces of fences, shop windows and street walls. Sides of train cars and an occasional ship became the surfaces for movable billboards of revolutionary propaganda. One very effective method in reaching the illiterate masses was the poster series (ROSTA Windows) issued by the Russian Telegraph Agency that drew on the population's familiarity with prerevolutionary vernacular woodcuts, picture story broadsides and the motifs of the religious icon painting tradition as the basis for its style. The ROSTA artists utilized the technology of this electric form of communication to quickly spread the images from a central creative studio in Moscow to ROSTA locations throughout the Soviet territories. Incidentally, the official TASS news agency revived this tradition after World War II.

Obviously, having to be simultaneously traditional and radical can set one up to use old iconic images to spread a new gospel, so to speak, and can have some unintended consequences. One of the ironies of drawing on traditional motifs that the masses would be familiar with as a springboard for communicating the revolution's goals was reported by Arthur Ransome on a visit to Moscow in 1919. He noticed that on the Kremlin gates near a chapel, "Religion is the Opium of the Masses" had been placed in a small frame not unlike the style typical for the display of sacred icons. He reported that he saw many people going into the chapel, evidently unable to read, cross themselves reverently before the revolutionary inscription, without any regard to the mockery of the new regime of anything religious (Ibid., 112).

Designing the poster image was a way for artists to commit themselves to the revolution so that artists from various stylistic directions became increasingly involved in the production of optimistic images of revolutionary utopianism. Posters exalting the troops in the civil war years (1918–1922) varied in style from *Beat the Whites with the Red Wedge* (1920), an avant-garde style image by El Lissittsky consisting of dynamically opposed geometric shapes and a text (illustration 27), to Dmitri Moor's *Have You Enrolled as a Volunteer?* (1920), a naturalistically rendered soldier in a bright red uniform pointing at the audience (illustration 10) in the manner of James Montgomery Flagg's famed Uncle Sam recruiting poster for World War I (illustration 11). Most of the military poster publications were created under the auspices of Leon Trotsky, the People's Commissar for Military and Naval Affairs (1918–1925), where boldly defined soldiers and peasants were often depicted heroically moving forward in solidarity toward the Red Star of revolutionary purpose (just think of the image of a star, far away but inspiring to all those who look up to the sky).

The "fine arts" shared this desire as well, to manifest the promise of the revolution in visual terms. But the avant-garde style of geometric abstraction typical to the experimental art of the prerevolutionary aesthetics of Suprematism (Malevich), Cubo-Futurism (Gonachorva), and Constructivism (Tatlin and Rodchenko) began to arouse objection from supporters of traditional representational imagery in both the artistic and government circles. Art historians associated with the government publication of posters for the military argued for realistic rather than abstract work. Workers, soldiers, and peasants drawn in squares, circles, and triangles were senseless images that couldn't express the integrity of the revolution. Complicated allegory, even if it used realistic images, was just as problematic for these officials as it was deemed too open to the possibility of multiple or varying interpretations that couldn't be controlled in one specific direction. Public decorations in the avant-garde manner, often referred to by Pravda reviewers as "the fashionable futuristic style," met with opposition as being incomprehensible and condemned as a mockery of the taste of the working class. Marc Chagall's decorations for the 1919 celebration in Vitebsk (his hometown) of the first anniversary of the revolution that included banners with images of flying green cows were severely criticized as a "mystical and formalistic bacchanal" that wasted public revenue and were under no circumstances proletarian art (Ibid., 133).

Theorizing about the appropriate character of art in a proletarian society led many artists to argue that "art," in any traditional sense, irrespective of its style, was part of the spiritual culture of the past, and therefore trying to express Marxist social theory was aesthetically doomed to whither away in a collectivist society. Traditional easel paintings and sculptures were considered to be opposed to the State's political agenda. Art in a communist world should not depict but change it, as Feuerbach's eleventh thesis suggested, and the avant-garde came to the conclusion that only a radically redefined Constructivism or what quickly became labeled as Productionism would be the appropriate path for the artist to undertake in this new society. The only valid aesthetic would be one that combined art and the industrial process, one that moved from old-fashioned bourgeois appreciation of the subtle beauty of capitalist leisure and pretense to a means of human socialization and commitment to change. The way for the artist was clear: she or he had to become an artist/engineer. Artists would participate directly in the production process. How the ideal of the integration of art and technology, of exchange-value and use-value, social and technical utility for the public at large as well as the artistic community, should be implemented became a heated debate in the artistic world of Russia in the 1920s. Of course, there were those who advocated the opposing position that art should have a spiritual and poetic purpose or just be art for art's sake, but they had to flee to Western Europe. The Production Artists immediately strove to respond to this ideological goal. Functionalism was the conception that guided the textiles, dishes, furniture, posters, and interior design, and Productionism set the conditions for moving the artist from the easel to the machine. If artists were to be workers too, and if they were to contribute to the new classless society, then they ought to justify their functional existence and their role in the transformation of the state and the pursuit of the ideals of communism by reshaping everyday objects and the environment in which the proletariat worked and lived. These creative objects were literally weapons for establishing the revolutionary culture and paving the way for the glories of a collective future.

One could observe in the formation and development of the Soviet Union how artists lost their privileged position of an elite community of creators, and turned into "workers" who accomplished tasks, and worked collectively to bring about a better society in which to live. As such, they had to contribute their talents for the greater good of the whole, and not enjoy celebrity status or personal gratification. The great contribution of such a shift in conception is that it forced individuals to think in terms of the community in which they lived, and it also forced to them to engage with the issues of the day, such as industrial production and military fortification. Similarly, it forced generations of artists to expand their aesthetic horizons from the limited confines of the French Salon or museum, for example, into the crafts and sciences, such as furniture, architecture, textiles, and factory production. Yes, individual creativity might have been stifled; yes, personal tastes were truncated; but likewise personal greed and arrogance were truncated and stifled, because artists bought into the ideal that the community as a whole took precedence over the individual. These ideals were understood in universal terms, and therefore we move now to examine what happened on another continent around the same time, Mexico.

In the fall of 1927, the International Transport Workers Union arranged for Diego Rivera, a Mexican artist and member of the Communist Party, to visit the USSR to participate in the tenth anniversary of the October Revolution. Rivera was among a group of mural painters who had risen to prominence after the 1910 revolution in Mexico. We should note here that just as posters were the primary medium for Soviet political art of the early twentieth century, with their public displays and accessibility, so were murals in the Soviet Union and in Mexico. Likewise, the content of their art had an accessible nationalistic concern as these mural painters were dedicated to expressing the ideals and history of the Mexican Revolution and emphasizing the values of the indigenous heritage of their country. While not exclusively so, the majority of these artists espoused socialist or communist political ideals and as such were antifascist, anti-imperialist, and antimilitaristic. Rivera was no exception as he was an active political leader of labor groups in his homeland and a skillful anti-imperialist polemicist. Although closely linked to the Communist Party, Rivera was always a "maverick" or "ultraleftist" who refused to go along uncritically with the party line (Craven 1997, 97).

By the time Rivera arrived in Moscow, he was credited with the accomplishment of the Ministry of Education Murals (Secretaria de Education Publica) in Mexico City, thus establishing his reputation worldwide. The mural series on the walls and in the stairways of the ministry building was begun in 1923, shortly after Rivera had returned to his native country having spent the previous twelve years in study and art making among the avant-garde of Europe. An ardent believer in the Leninist revolutionary movement, he returned to Mexico after this exposure to European modernist art to dedicate himself to portraying the history of his country with a politically radical vision. The manifesto of the Union of Technical Workers, Painters, and Sculptors that he joined in 1922 proclaimed: "We repudiate the so-called easel painting and all the art of ultra-intellectual circles, because it is aristocratic and we glorify the expression of Monumental Art (mural images) because it is a public possession" (Hurlburt 1991, 53). It is evident that these mural artists were dedicated to the proposition that art should be public and available to the masses, and not remain just the private property of wealthy collectors. Just as posters took over as the medium of choice of the Soviet regime, so murals took over as the medium of choice of the new Mexican revolutionary forces.

While trained in the iconography and fresco techniques of the Italian Renaissance mural tradition, Riviera would transform in his own work what were primarily art projects whose major accomplishments (Michelangelo's Sistine Ceiling, Giotto's Arena Chapel, and Raphael's Vatican Apartments, for instance) were commissioned for private spaces by elitist patrons and unavailable to the masses. Rivera was committed, by contrast, to create popular mural imagery that would be available to the public and that would embrace the values of the pre-European culture of Mexico. The ideological content in Rivera's murals drew on the pre-Christian Conquest traditions of Latin America with the intention of awakening a consciousness of nationalism born in Mexico's indigenous heritage so as to reject the Eurocentricism he saw as the legacy of Mexico's colonial past. Rivera envisioned his artistic work as a vehicle for popular self-empowerment and awakening rather than merely populist rhetoric to fan the fires of the revolutionary regime. His commitment was to the living multicultural reality of Mexico, and not an affirmation of the myths of the official "tourist culture" centered on folk festivities and temples of "blood sacrifice." He rendered these ideals in bold colors using a drawing style that gave his figures a massive, monumental quality that innovatively combined the European Classicism of his artistic training with the Aztec and Mayan art that he consciously emulated.

His established stature as an internationally known muralist was acknowledged by his hosts at the Moscow School of Fine Arts, and upon arrival in Russia he was given a commission to paint murals for the Red Army Club. He aligned himself with the *October Group*, Russian artists who advocated for public art that promoted social ideals but whose style was based on vernacular aesthetic traditions. They were opposed to representational styles based in Classicism, the abstraction of the avant-garde, and the engineer/artist ideal of Art in Production. The artists of this group considered the aesthetic sensibilities of the masses to be seriously crippled by what they referred to as the "pseudo art of capitalist societies" (Azuela 2002, 127). However, *October* shared the Productionist goal that art would create the conditions necessary for the construction of a new collective society, namely, an art form that would be at the service of the workers and peasants in the international class struggle. The artists would consider themselves workers in the field of culture who labor in public service and contribute to define the very image of the worker in the new Communist society.

Rivera could not resist criticizing Stalin's politics, and openly expressed objection to his totalitarian policies especially in regard to the banning and exile of artists. The promised mural commission never materialized, and in May of 1828 the government asked him to return to Mexico under the pretense that his talent was needed for murals in his homeland. By 1932 Stalin officially banned all artistic expressions except Socialist Realism. It was at that point that Rivera's identification with Leon Trotsky began and continued until his assassination in Mexico City. His link with Trotsky, who was exiled from the USSR in 1929 and later admitted to Mexico with Rivera's help, went beyond mere displays of anti-Stalinist solidarity. They shared the same assessment of the Socialist Realism program for the arts, and Trotsky often repeated verbatim Rivera's critical assessment that after 1932 Soviet art was in the hands of "the old and bad academic painters," using "the worst techniques of bourgeois art." In a 1938 essay where Trotsky compared Stalinist art with Rivera, he stated that:

> The official art of the Soviet Union resembles totalitarian justice . . . The style of presenting official Soviet painting is called "socialist realism" . . . This "realism" consists in the imitation of provincial daguerreotypes of the

third quarter of the last century; the socialist character apparently consists of representing, in the manner of pretentious photography, events that never took place . . . the art of the Stalinist period will remain as the frankest expression of the profound decline of the proletarian revolution. (Craven 2002, 146)

Trotsky goes on in this essay to point to the murals of Rivera as evidence of a viable revolutionary art. The legitimate expression of the proletarian ideal was integral to Rivera's artistic method and imagery from Trotsky's perspective. The images of murals with these qualities paved the way toward the establishment of a harmonious, classless society, run by the workers of the world.

It would seem to be a complete contradiction that an artist with such an active Communist background would be commissioned to paint a mural in a Stock Exchange (San Francisco) and enjoy the patronage of an important industrialist family from the capitalist United States, such as the Rockefellers, but that was exactly what unfolded for Rivera in the 1930s. Rivera had a genial and unassuming manner, and while his presentation of his left-wing politics was candid it was seldom strident (Ibid., 131). These personal qualities combined with the wit, charm, and talent of his wife and fellow artist, Frida Kahlo, and the political clout of his American patrons helped to smooth over many of the objections that capitalist culture had to the lifelong partisan of the left. In spite of success with the first four commissions in the United States, the fifth, the Rockefeller Center murals, were cancelled and subsequently destroyed while Rivera was in the process of their completion. His refusal to remove a figure of Lenin not included in the review of the drawings for the project by the Rockefeller family initiated the conflict. The inclusion of this figure was an affront to the patrons who at the least would have had to face what would be the inevitable disapproval of their financial partners and risk the collapse of the entire Rockefeller Center project.

The *Detroit Industry* mural cycle for the Detroit Institute of Art courtyard that was commissioned during the Great Depression was completed while guards were actually shooting striking workers at the River Rouge plant of the Ford Motor Company. The contrast between glorified images of the working class and their emancipatory promises and the reality of the treatment of workers in factories was striking. People of all races are shown working side by side in harmony, while their individuality is maintained; the industrial complex is daunting, but there is a sense of accomplishment and appreciation of the final stages of capitalism (before communism takes over). Rivera expresses in the murals an awe of the technology and productivity of the United States economy that echoes sentiments of Marx from the *Communist Manifesto*:

> The bourgeoisie, during its scarce one hundred years, has created more massive and more colossal productive forces than have all preceding generations together . . . what earlier century had even a presentiment that such productive forces slumbered in the lap of social labor? (Marx 1988, 59)

Similar sentiments for political expression come out of the different traditions of revolutionary forces in the Soviet Union and in Mexico. As we said earlier, ours is not an attempt to provide a political and historical survey of revolutionary forces in the twentieth century, nor an attempt to illustrate how some of them, especially in the Soviet Union, Germany, and Italy turned into fascist regimes. By fascist, we mean those kinds of political structures and institutions where a totalitarian regime takes over and transcends the public-political arena into every facet of the private domain, where personal views and privacy are exposed to police surveillance in the name of national security and public safety. The reason why we are even interested in this political transformation of an ideology that seems inspiring and humane is that it can be seen in the twofold relationship between the artistic community and the political authorities as well as read through the artifacts produced during that time. The artifacts are then considered propaganda: an embodiment of the manipulation of an ideology in the hands of bureaucrats and forceful political agents.

In a short essay on anti-Semitism and Fascist propaganda, Theodor Adorno reminds us of the kind of analysis one ought to undertake in order to appreciate the "logic" or "rationality" of such activities. Being of the neo-Marxist Frankfurt School, Adorno was concerned to find structural and rational foundations according to which to analyze specific situations or institutions. Thinking about how fascist propaganda affected European culture in the past century, he reminds his readers that "Fascism habitually goes *beyond* what it has announced." That makes sense to him, because "Totalitarianism means knowing no limits, not allowing for any breathing spell, conquest with absolute domination, complete extermination of the chosen foe" (Adorno 1994, 164). This definition of the totalitarian mindset leads Adorno to explain how fascism operates: for him it sets up imaginary foes, sets them up in order to tear them to pieces, in his words "without caring much how this imagery is related to reality." In doing so, "it does not employ discursive logic but is rather . . . what might be called an organized flight of ideas" (Ibid., 165) Adorno's statements are useful in explaining the need to focus on visual, imaginary constructs in the political arena. The way ideology works, the way propaganda works, is linked to how people can be manipulated or deceived into accepting a fictitious image rather than discuss or critically analyze reality, facts, actual people and their behavior, or rational ideas that are substantiated by an argument or empirical evidence.

III: THE ARTISTIC FACES OF DEMOCRACY (AND FASCISM)

In what follows, we'll focus on national myths as narratives we tell ourselves in order to foster a set of beliefs that bind us as a culture. But national myths, such as military heroism or religious freedom, require visual presentations that complement textual narratives. Undertaking either component, cultural workers (authors, poets, poster designers, and propagandists alike) face the following predicament: though their appeal is on one level to some universal principles, such as beauty or heroism, on another level it must conform to and fit a particular national character, such as the conquest of the American Western front or American ingenuity. It's exactly this predicament that interests us: Is the American cultural narrative universal in its appeal or limited to a political agenda? This question has a certain contemporary urgency in the face of our invasion and occupation of Afghanistan and Iraq where we claim to promote democratic principles that should have a universal appeal despite the specific American undertones with which they are applied.

What brings the fascism of the communist promise to bear on the American experience is the manner in which folklorist visual cues were jettisoned in favor of industrialization and images of the machine. It is in this sense that any and all political parties around the world embraced technoscientific progress and the promises it embodied so as to deliver their people from feudal abuse of power, starvation, disease, and illiteracy. Could we, then, argue that what fascism and democracy, totalitarianism, socialism, communism, and capitalism have in common is a thirst for industrialization? Once phrased in this way, obviously, we endorse the conflation between economic, social, and political systems. For if we were more pedantic, we would insist that capitalism were matched with socialism, democracy with totalitarianism, and so on. But since we accept the premises of Adam Smith (1776) and Karl Marx (1844 ff.) alike, both of whom claimed that the economic conditions of a society determine its social and political (moral and legal) character and frameworks, it is easy to slide from one framework to the other, appreciating their intricate and mutual influence. To endorse individualism, let's say, is to endorse an economic system of competition among individuals in the free and equally accessible marketplace. However, such endorsement prefigures the need for political, social, and legal protections and incentives so that the individual (anonymous as she or he must remain) will be able to succeed (or at least believe that success is tenable). Likewise, to endorse collectivism is to endorse an economic system of cooperation among individuals in a coordinated and planned state. However, such an endorsement (like its counterpart) prefigures the need for political, social, and legal protections and incentives so that the individual will be able to live peacefully.

If either case were to be followed by anyone, it must have an appeal to the individuals under consideration. Why would an individual be swayed to follow the one rather than the other? We suggest here that the crucial element in appealing to and convincing individuals to follow one set of ideas or another has to do with their presentations, what myths they construct and how they "sell" them. Selling them, so to speak, is a form of projection that requires symbols and visual aids in order to simplify them to the extreme and make them as accessible as possible to the greatest number of people. We doubt that anyone who was trying to make a living in the twentieth century and survive the pressures of an ensuing industrial revolution would have had the time or inclination to read either masterpiece of Smith or Marx (hundreds and thousands of impenetrable pages of dense prose that make our own writing readable by comparison). Yes, a picture is indeed worth a thousand words!

Just as there is a national pressure under fascism, there is a similar ideological pressure under democracy. This is true especially if we accept, with Robert Paxton (2005), that to speak of fascism is to speak about many different things at once. Just as we cannot simply talk about totalitarianism, since each twentieth-century variant has come up with its own version, such as a militaristic one in Chile under Allende with a capitalist economy of the Chicago style (Milton Friedman and company), as opposed to the Stalinist version with a strong political apparatus that micromanaged the economy and every aspect of the public and private life of its citizens and claimed communism as the economic foundation of the new republic. Yes, in all cases the military plays a role (there is need for force and control), and yes, there is an appeal to the youth of the culture to jettison the past and embrace a wonderful novel future, but still each country has its own issues to deal with. Perhaps, as Paxton argues, there are similar needs for finding a common enemy (as Horkheimer and Adorno agree), Jews in one case, religious institutions in another, and always the self-interested and wealthy bourgeois (unless they help finance the changes brought about by a fascist regime).

Fascism, then, is of interest to Paxton in his analysis because the appeal isn't to a universal set of beliefs and ideas, but rather to a set of national, traditional myths and folktales. If the source of legitimation is founded on old traditions and folklike attitudes, then it's obvious why radical individualism of the capitalist and democratic sorts or the universalism of the communists would be suspect. But just as much as fascist regimes have relied on the past, they also found in the past some "enemies" or negative influences that prevented the spirit of power and authority, of pride and hope, to come through. It is in this sense, then, that Paxton opens the way for appreciating the evolutionary and developmental character of fascism (and refuses to find its essence or core). In their so-called antipolitical pretense, fascist movements were able to take over political institutions and redistribute power relations among different agencies and bureaucratic interests, radicalizing them as needed under different circumstances (sometimes against the monarchy, sometimes against the church, and always in tandem with the militias or military generals).

Similar concerns underlie what one can say about democracy. We move from direct, representational democracy to a democratic republicanism, from parliamentary to presidential, from proportional to indirect. Each twentieth-century variant has some features we highlight or ignore, find as strengths or weaknesses (see Cohen 1982). Since this isn't a discourse in political philosophy, we'll leave it open to multiple interpretations, but assume some common features that are highlighted, that pose similar ideological and visual opportunities to those wishing to "sell" the ideals of democracy. For those living in the United States, many questions concerning our constitutional democracy came into public notice after the 2000 presidential election. Some legal experts and political scientists, such as Robert Dahl (2003), explained in great detail why the Electoral College and the Senate were set in place, so as to remind us that we are a republic and not a democracy, a political arrangement with the appropriate institutions that would curtail public power and ensure the concentration of power in the hands of the aristocracy (understood economically and not hereditarily here, as opposed to some European countries).

If we'd examine, for example, any of these questions visually rather than philosophically, then we'd find different ways of analyzing the attitudes and images associated with these ideas. Moreover, once these kinds of debates come about, someone must produce images that exemplify, express, and embody the ideas being fought over. We'd like to illustrate the (similar) pressure under which artists are put in order to produce their works and be able to sell them in the marketplace (of ideas and of capitalism alike). The areas are propagandalike in their insistence on delivering a message to the masses that is easily understood and can be acted on: the military (war effort and heroism), labor organization (unions or individual), capitalist production and consumption (with advertisement for products), and the pastoral West (manifest destiny and rugged individualism). We'd like to show how similar the artistic faces of democracy are to those of fascism when it gets to images and ideological messages sent through these images. The reason for undertaking this comparison is to explain the predicament under which artists work, regardless of national boundaries or ideological commitments. It's also to highlight the internal confusions in American ideology—labor as individuated and as a group effort, military as personal heroism and collaborative effort—as well as their parallels with allegedly opposing ideologies—of the communists and fascists, or the totalitarian regimes and their dictatorial powers.

The predicament of artists has been and will always remain their own complicity (explicitly or implicitly) in the affairs of the state while maintaining a critical attitude. What we have called elsewhere (Sassower and Cicotello 2000) their detached attachment is a balancing act that can be condemned as politically naïve if not an outright sellout. Is it possible to find a spiritual moment in art that is both sublime and universal? Is it possible to avoid any and all political influences? Just as there is a national pressure under fascism to represent the dreams and hopes of an emerging ideology with particular cultural matrices (for example, overthrowing a monarchy or a feudal autocracy), there is a similar ideological pressure under democracy to explain to the people at large exactly what is meant by liberty and equality (for example, turning the issue of equality in to equal opportunity in the second half of the twentieth century). Compare the *Lincoln Memorial* with a *Stalin Memorial* of the same period; likewise, there is an interesting comparison between the colossal heads of George Washington and Benito Mussolini. (See illustrations 12–15).

In this sense, then, there is a propagandalike demeanor in underwriting, promoting, subsidizing, and distributing images that would evoke hope and pride in the minds and hearts of those committed to this form of government. Though democratic in nature and seemingly free of the kind of censorship ascribed to totalitarian regimes, we should note here that there is still insistence on delivering a message to the masses that is easily understood, that remains unambiguous, inspiring, and that can be acted on.

As we go through the following four themes, we'd like to show how similar the artistic faces of democracy are to those of fascism when it gets to putting them out there for public consumption, when they are expressed in posters and murals, in venues that are not limited to museums and galleries (as the venues of critical and connoisseur appreciation).

1. *War Effort:* patriotism, fighting for freedom, independence, the pursuit of happiness; glorious victories exacted in the eighteenth century from the British crown, and in the twentieth century from Japanese imperialism and European fascism. Some of the most artistically sophisticated poster images in twentieth-century American art were created to bolster various war efforts. The appeal is to patriotic values that stress the

goal of fighting for freedom and protecting American independence. The appeal to women to share in the responsibilities of the war effort was often featured. In the WWII period, Norman Rockwell's *Rosie the Riveter* of 1943 (see illustration 20) and other muscular women (see illustration 9, *We Can Do It!* poster) were depicted as fully capable of doing the hard work necessary to ensure domestic support for our soldiers abroad. It's interesting to note in this context that though feminist concerns appear much later in American culture, there is already a nascent appreciation of the value of female labor and the potential contribution to any national goal. (Note captioned posters from the World War I era that said "Gee, if I were a man I would join [the navy]." Today it is "Be All You Can Be" for both genders and in all branches of the armed services.) Who can forget the boldly rendered Uncle Sam pointed his finger directly at the potential recruit with a commanding "I want you for U.S. Army" in the 1917 James Montgomery Flagg poster, illustration 11 (see comparison with a counterpart in D. S. Moor's Bolshevik poster, illustration 10).

2. *Labor:* the right to work, the pride of working to earn a living and provide for one's family; being part of a group or a community of workers; creating something out of nothing, especially with the natural riches and resources of America; equal opportunity to climb the corporate ladder; freedom to pursue any career, enterprise, idea. Work is as valuable in American ideology as in any Rivera mural. The Federal Art Project of the 1930s' Work Progress Administration (WPA) sponsored *America Today* murals of Thomas Hart Benton that provided a panorama of American workers toiling heroically in a multitude of activities, ranging from urban construction of skyscrapers, aviation, and mining workers to rural cotton picking and cattle ranching. This pride associated with these images is related, of course, to one's national efforts, both domestic and internationally: keep America strong and independent! Strongly muscular and burly workers exuding the capacity for endless, committed labor are proudly depicted, and as we can tell, can be easily transformed into brave soldiers who will defend these occupations and ideals. Wholesome, homespun rural values are featured in the farming couple featured in Grant Wood's painting *"American Gothic."* Poster titles, such as *Work to Keep Free, Work for America* summarize the ideological goals of putting America's labor resources to their appropriate and moral purpose (see illustrations 16–19 that compare a hammer in the strong arm

of the laborer, Soviet, Italian, Mexican, and American; see also illustrations 20–21 of American female laborers. Images such as these which celebrate the contributions of working women have parallel depictions in every major political ideology.

3. *Capitalism, Commercialism, and the Marketplace:* individualism, entrepreneurship, motivation and ambition, competition and success, ownership of private property; freedom and equality reinforced in the market economy where no barriers block access or eventual success, where there is built-in personal pride and satisfaction in accomplishing what one set out to do. The freedom of the capitalist marketplace with its ideals of entrepreneurship, the opportunity for the individual to succeed in a competitive environment through his or her own motivation and ambition, comes to life with a great deal of images produced by and distributed through marketing agencies and advertising cartels. Images of the freedom and equality made possible by the market economy as it serves to nurture the democratic ideal are the basis for selling any product at any cost. There is, of course, the Andy Warhol irony of appreciating the social leveling effect of a Coca-Cola bottle that is equally accessible (and costs about the same amount of money) no matter if you are a laborer or a farmer, a soldier or the president of the United States. (Illustrations in this area are common and difficult to reproduce because of copyright issues—just check your local magazine stand and poster shop for lively examples.)

4. *The Pastoral West:* rugged individualism, Yankee ingenuity, the gold rush and wealth—exploring and mining for gold and silver, open spaces and unhindered horizons, open to new opportunities. In the nineteenth century the drive of Manifest Destiny broadens the borders of the United States and establishes the West as a land with mythical promise of riches and potential new economic opportunities (see illustration 9 of John Gast's *American Progress,* the personification of Manifest Destiny's parade westward). Landscape artists inform the society "back East" of the progress of this ideal with glorious images often painted from the very trains that began to crisscross the formerly wild terrain. In the beginning of the twentieth century, majestic scenery and indigenous cultures of the West became the stuff of tourist legend and the vistas of national parks. Sure enough, these images were revisited in a commercialized form by the middle of the past century in newly developed arts communities that became the playgrounds of the rich, such as Santa Fe, New Mexico; Aspen, Colorado; and Jackson Hole, Wyoming.

The reason for delineating these four themes is to explain three sets of predicaments facing artists who work within the context of the American version of democracy. First, just because our variant of democracy is familiar and has been internalized over two hundred years does not keep it immune to criticism. What we take for granted may be flawed; what we have been indoctrinated to believe in may be problematic both theoretically and in its practical applications. So, artists, like other citizens, have the predicament of questioning the ideological cave in which they were brought up. Like Socrates at his trial, they have to accept the political structures in which they live (implicitly if not explicitly) and the benefits associated with these structures and institutions they have enjoyed throughout their life, while being critical and opposed to their principles and abuses of power.

Second, though living in a democracy, and though believing that by comparison to fascism and totalitarianism democracy is superior in any political, social, economic, and moral sense, artists provide a service for their culture and for their state. They remain beholden to the power of the state and its coffers, and therefore must subconsciously (if not openly) promote the value of their ideology. They become part of a propaganda machine despite the fact that they work independently and sell their wares in the open market. In some perverse sense, they cannot escape the trappings and allure, the medals and honors, the financial and cultural rewards bestowed on those patriotic soldiers on the march to cultural victory.

And third, though yearning on some level to be critical of their surroundings and provide a spiritual outlet for their creativity and the aspirations of others, artists are always bound by the cultural context in which they work. Is it possible to strip any image of some cultural clues or references? Is there indeed a universal appeal that transcends national and cultural boundaries? Or have the universal images been claimed with specific elitist pretensions that claim for themselves the right to dictate what is beautiful or sublime? So, if artists remain nationalistic despite themselves, aren't they better off just admitting their prejudices, acknowledging their allegiance, and disclaiming any artistic value outside the mighty dollar or the warm refuge of police protection?

The next chapter is devoted to an examination of the universal elements to which artists appeal regardless of the national identities they must assume or the ideological convictions they must express in their works. The aesthetic expressions of a national identity would wash away if they remain dependent on a universal aesthetic appeal; what would the difference be, then? This paradoxical condition is examined in the following chapter.

8

9

ТЫ
ЗАПИСАЛСЯ
ДОБРОВОЛЬЦЕМ?

10

I WANT YOU
FOR U.S. ARMY
NEAREST RECRUITING STATION

11

12

13

14

15

WORK TO KEEP FREE!

16

17

12-27
APRILE
1934-XII
XV FIERA
DI MILANO
RIDUZIONE

18

19

THE SATURDAY EVENING
POST
MAY 29, 1943   10¢
BEGINNING—A NEW
KELLAND SERIAL
Heart on Her Sleeve
EDGAR SNOW
REPORTS ON GERMAN
ATROCITIES
ROSIE
Norman Rockwell

20

The Girl on the Land
Serves the Nation's Need
apply Y.W.C.A.
Land Service Committee.

21

3

THE UNIVERSAL FACES OF ART

I: REDUCTIONISM IN THE NAME OF UNIVERSALISM

As we have seen in the previous chapter, there are similar aesthetic elements that appeared in the propaganda materials of democratic and fascist regimes during the twentieth century. It's not only that some specific images of strength and courage, power and resolve (the hammer, for example) have the same appeal across national boundaries, but that they almost speak to us or are read by us as if the grammar and the vocabulary of the visual language (what Nelson Goodman [1976] calls "the languages of art") are clearly understood. One could think in this context of Noam Chomsky (2000) and his group of linguists who argue that the human mind is "hardwired" in the same way so that languages, however seemingly different, arise out of the same basis and therefore are translatable across the linguistic landscape. This way of thinking about humans and their cognitive apparatus has led some to speculate on an even grander or more profound level.

Both Noel Carroll and Ronald de Sousa suggest that there is an evolutionary foundation that explains the similar cognitive and emotive reaction to visual images across national and geographical boundaries. The reason there is a similarity, according to them, is that humans have developed adaptive mechanisms that allowed them to evolve in particular ways. Put differently, humans used aesthetically appealing images and visual representations so as to structure and explain the world around them, and that process ensured their survival over thousands of years. Just as J. J. Gibson (1966) argued about the adaptive visual framing and perception of the frog that spots flies as food and of pilots who orient themselves according to the terrain, so do these two suggest that art, in the general sense we appreciate it, plays this role for humans. Gibson's so-called theory of information pickup suggests that perception depends entirely upon information in the "stimulus array" rather than sensations that are influenced by cognition. Gibson proposes that the environment consists of affordances (such as terrain, water, vegetation, etc.) that provide the clues necessary for perception. According to Gibson, perception is a direct consequence of the properties of the environment and does not involve any form of sensory processing. Appreciating the interactive elements in perception, he still puts more emphasis on external stimuli in comparison to the "internal" structural elements suggested by Carroll and de Sousa. Of course, on some level of analysis this is a difference in degrees of influence, not in kind (because of their mutual influences).

There are some issues we must outline at this juncture so as to consider this way of thinking. To begin with, we should reconsider what we mean by art. There are three general paths along the definition and classification of art. First, one can recount and survey artifacts, objects, artworks, material items deemed artistic, or even a wider range of "things" we can appreciate as having an aesthetic value, being "beautiful" in some sense of the term. It helps to distinguish them if they lack a use-value (in Marx's sense), so that their appearance and exchange become for their sake alone, without an overt consumption. This would include frescoes and paintings, sculptures and vases, as well as natural objects and phenomena, such as waterfalls and rainbows, landscapes and eclipses. In all of these cases, there is an "it" that is encountered with one of our senses.

The second way to talk about art is to talk about its constitutive qualities that defy definition, that turn it into the sublime. Whether understood in Kantian terms of the sublime or Lyotard's notion of the "unspeakable," what we have before us cannot be classified other than to say that it's beyond our material classification, beyond verbal definitions, outside the realm of the known. It therefore could be a spiritual or transcendental object that in its profundity loses the standard characteristics of any object.

The third way to talk about art is to talk of the aesthetic experience, namely, the actions and reactions that come about when encountering what is loosely defined as art. Here we add a human component to the object, so that we appreciate the interactive nature of the experience, and therefore are moved to analyze emotions rather than thoughts, expressions rather than ideas. Along this line of analysis, there is something unique about the aesthetic experience as compared with all other experiences. It evokes certain parts of our psyche and provokes certain reactions that require a different vocabulary from the one we use to analyze our ideas and cognition, our thoughts and arguments. It's unclear whether this set of reactions and emotive responses taps into an individual or collective unconscious; it's also unclear how deep or superficial these responses are, and whether they can be manipulated or not, whether they are raw or artificially constructed.

It's the third way of talking about art that seems to support the views expressed by Carroll and de Sousa. For Carroll, for example, it's really about human nature rather than about this or that piece of art. As he says, "to a rather surprising degree, the artworks of foreign societies are cross-culturally recognizable as artworks and that calls for an explanation. And since the phenomenon is cross-cultural and not explicable in terms of merely cultural diffusion, the invocation of human nature appears irresistible." What Carroll is looking for, then, is not merely a vague or abstract notion or appreciation of human nature, but a more robust notion of the "relevant, enduring features of our cognitive, perceptual, and emotive architecture." But in order not to appear too reductionist in his view, namely, in order not to jettison a cultural and historical explanation for a biological one, Carroll admits that these two perspectives can be mutually informative and influence each other during their evolutionary development. As he says, "in some cases psychology, including evolutionary psychology, may enrich historical explanations" (Carroll 2004, 96). But what is the "architecture" of which Carroll speaks? For him that is what explains our aesthetic experiences, that which has evolved in humans over generations, since "art, especially of our traditional, transcultural variety, addresses our evolved sensibilities, feelings, emotions, and perceptual faculties in a fairly direct manner, while also depending on activating relatively basic cognitive and imaginative capabilities, such as the ability to follow narratives and to entertain fictions" (Ibid., 99).

If Carroll provides the broader framework for thinking about the evolution of aesthetic sensibilities in humans as necessary components for development and survival, de Sousa provides more detailed arguments. While reviewing Ellen Dissayanake's stronger view of the biological nature of art, its essential function in the evolution of humanity, and claiming that art is "genetically innate," he suggests that she may have gone too far in her arguments. He also mentions Frederick Turner's weaker proposals that "art served our ancestors in navigating the world in practice," and the more "ambitious thesis" that "art actually reveals to us the deep structure of the laws of the universe" (de Sousa 2004, 110–1). Perhaps there is a way to discuss the important function that art plays in communication, for example, or in exploration of humans over time without claiming to expose an aesthetic gene on which humans depend for their survival or a direct causal connection between artistic images and the laws of nature.

De Sousa ends up with a helpful classification of four kinds of biological functions that one could attribute to art and artifacts, even to the aesthetic experience humans learned to pay attention to over the years. The first he calls "beauty as a solution to a coordination problem," by which he means the informational component of art in our cognitive appreciation and comprehension of diverse experiences and encounters. The second he calls "beauty as the phenomenal correlate of non-standard mechanism of selection," by which he means the kind of "sexual selection" that explains natural selection in aesthetic terms. The third he calls "beauty as a reflection of the innate structure of the universe," by which he means the kind of deep structure that the mind evolved to have and that can understand the world in which humans live. The fourth and last he calls "beauty as the pleasure taken in the exercise of the cognitive mechanisms of the brain," by which he means the kind of "play" the mind enjoys and therefore maintains and perpetuates, regardless of all the other physical constraints (Ibid., 116–7).

Any of these explanations that transcend the boundaries of the physical components of human evolution or the mutual influence of the body and mind (in Cartesian terms or any, more contemporary ones of cognitive psychology and artificial intelligence) make biologists, such as Richard Lewontin uncomfortable. For him, a biological theory of human nature that attempts to find certain "inborn similarities among all of us," reeks of and can lead to the "ideology of biological determinism" (Lewontin 1991, 23). Once the study of biology is understood in ideological terms, namely, as a human activity that has a political agenda attached to it (to explain why some individuals are necessarily more successful than others and therefore legitimate their differences), then questions about causal relations between genes and organisms or between organisms and the environment in which they survive might be answered more fruitfully. For him, then, to speak of an "art gene" that determines a certain outcome of human evolution is to speak erroneously. Any direct, determined, causal relation cannot be mapped out, since humans create their own environments and those environments impact them as well; it's a mutual interaction all the way "down" or "up" the evolutionary ladder, regardless of the units of analysis.

So, what motivates those who argue about the so-called art gene? At the root of this inclination is the desire to find an explanatory model that could encompass cross-cultural diversity, as Carroll insists. But are they indeed talking about the same thing? Is it an aesthetic experience they attempt to capture or the visual detection of artifacts? Are all artifacts apprehended cognitively and emotively alike? Are they even considered so by everyone? We know that some of us view the same things differently or would fail to recognize anything aesthetic in what someone else heralds as a work of art. We also know that our reactions differ when confronted by the same objects; yet, do we all have some reaction, some response? And if we do, can't that be a sufficient ground to make the claim that in fact we are similar, after all?

Perhaps if we shift back to Goodman's view on the languages of art, we might see something that could answer some of these questions. Assume, then, that we no longer speak the language of genes, the popular reductionist turn in contemporary science and culture to ascertain once and for all who is responsible for what. Instead, let's turn to a broader framework that motivates such determinism. For us, there is an ideological commitment here to the ethos of certainty. Within this ideological commitment, determinism and universalism make perfect sense. They draw their intellectual support from, among others, Descartes' radical doubt in his quest for certainty: we want to know for sure that this is the case. Twentieth-century variants of this quest can be seen in the development of probability theory and statistics, tools with which to view diverse phenomena and the incomplete collection of data within predictable patterns (emergence theory and chaos theory likewise find patterns and propensities, models and paths). As we cannot leave the world as an incomprehensible mess, we'd like to organize it and understand the principles by which it works. We even venture to describe the laws of nature, and when we push further (with or without religious zeal) we even ascribe to ourselves universal features and characteristics we call human nature. Staying within this framework of what can be called a speculative scientific domain (because the evidence for, or the verification or falsification of, these claims remain unclear and somewhat vague at this stage), one can argue that if we can detect universal elements, then we can also tap into them. How we tap into them and for what reasons, become central questions to discuss in the next section.

II: NEURATH'S ISOTYPES

Let's remember that what we are concerned with in this book is the political dimension of the artistic process of creation and dissemination, a process that cannot be simply relegated to the capitalist mode of exchange, where the marketplace alone dictates tastes and prices. Instead, there are layers of overlapping communities that mutually influence each other and direct the flow of information and capital, that set in motion certain activities that otherwise would not come about. By the time you figure out who decides what and for what reasons it may be too late to change the course of events. This is true for politicians running for office who are financed by certain groups that have the power to influence the fate of an election. This is true for manufacturers who are trying to bring a new product to the market and influence behavior patterns that might benefit from this product or may reject it outright. And obviously this is true of the artistic community, understood here to include the advertising industry and teaching institutions, artists who sell through galleries and in community fairs, as well as those who directly work for corporate America.

It is against this background, and with the kind of ideological aspiration suggested in the previous section in regard to (deterministic) science that we move back in history to the Vienna Circle of the period between the two World Wars (a group of intellectuals and natural philosophers). The case of Otto Neurath and his Social and Economic Museum in Vienna (founded in 1924) provides an informative example with which to discuss these issues. Though the Vienna Circle itself was made up of a group of intellectuals who might have had political convictions outside their trade (socialist or otherwise), the group deeply worried about a uniform representation of nature and a rule-bound linguistic apparatus with which to communicate sense-data. One could even say that the Vienna Circle could be thought of as apolitical because of its philosophical commitments to rid language of its metaphysical trappings and meaningless expressions (an objective and neutral language based on Protocol sentences) so as to turn communication into a method that is transparent (rather than opaque). As such, one could see through any attempt to manipulate words and ideas into convincing or ideologically loaded banters; one could immediately recognize (and scientifically verify) if what is said is true or false.

Neurath's museum, though, seemed to have had a very clear ideological agenda that used the ideas and practices of the Vienna "method," but that hoped to go beyond political neutrality. Neurath appreciated the fact that "modern man is conditioned by the cinema and a wealth of illustrations." He also acknowledged that the consumption of information happens "during leisure hours," and primarily visually. Instead of fighting this trend or finding it outside the realm of education or communication proper, Neurath suggested that we ought to work with these conditions and therefore "informative pictures and models should be part of a comprehensive whole. . . . Graphic representations of statistics should be made in such a way that they are not only correct but also fascinating." In a quick move, we are introduced to the need for aesthetic appeal when dealing with ideas and data, when trying to extend the economic, social, and political discourse to the general public (rather than keeping it within small groups of experts) (Neurath 1973, 214).

Neurath's rationale for the development of universal signs was explained in the following paragraph:

> Just through its neutrality, and its independence of separate languages, visual education is superior to word education. *Words divide, pictures unite.* The work of the Museum will become important in all forms of international information. (Ibid. 217)

The claims for the universal appeal and transparency of the symbols used in the charts of the museum are based on their neutrality in regard to the cues and embedded meanings we find in words and languages. Incidentally, the claim about international communication isn't as outlandish as it sounds, since one can find these symbols and signs nowadays in every airport around the globe, on a variety of products that are transported across national borders, and on the Internet when we can recognize icons and messages with a quick gesture of a sign. Yes, pictures do unite us in the sense we discussed in the previous section, as if there is a universal genetic field to which all human perceptions adhere. The only price for this direct educational impact, as far as Neurath was concerned, was the process of simplification, wherein some details are omitted so that the image will be remembered (see illustrations 23–25) (Ibid., 220).

Surely, there is a political agenda that can be attached to this method, since at its core it attempts to educate illiterates, for example, and to make data accessible to the largest number of citizens. There is an antielitist thrust and a deep commitment to public education in this method; there is a socialist or democratic mind-set behind such proposals. And the "international" flavor of Neurath's proclamation comes close to the communist platform of uniting the workers of the world and not merely enlisting national union membership here and there. Why bother to think internationally altogether? Either because we believe that we have similar human origins (human nature and genetics, as we examined above), or because we wish to bring all humans together (in a Hegelian, Marxist, or religious sense). Though neutral in a linguistic sense, though deprived of unintended connotations and misrepresentations, this method could be politically extremely useful. Put differently, if the symbols are themselves neutral in some broad sense, it would make the potential audience more susceptible and less skeptical in accepting the messages that these images conveyed. In short, they could be manipulated, which in turn means that they could be skillfully used for propaganda. It's not surprising that when the Nazis occupied Austria, one of the first places they took over in Vienna was this museum—what better tools could they find to tell their story, to weave their narrative of "liberation" and eternal hope?

And to some extent, the International System of TYpographic Picture Education provided the means of bridging the gap between the educated and uneducated, as Neurath understood them, and set up a "special visual dictionary and a special visual grammar" (Ibid., 224). But what is to be conveyed, what knowledge is to be transmitted with the use of this method? As far as Neurath was concerned,

> The term "knowledge" is often ambiguous; I use it to indicate a more or less connected group of statements and arguments of a factual kind, synonymous with empirical knowledge. That transfer of knowledge, i.e., of certain statements and arguments, becomes more universal and comprehensive is a characteristic of modern times. Since everybody is implicated in taking common decisions, directly or indirectly, the spreading of knowledge seems to be essential for the smooth working of democracy. (Ibid., 230)

From "factual knowledge" to democracy in one paragraph! The belief that knowledge is factual and that its broad dissemination would enhance the decision-making process in a democratic nation is itself an ideology (a set of beliefs and commitments both about humanity and about political systems). One could speculate that Wittgenstein would approve of the simplification of facts in a linguistic matrix, but might find the appeal of pictorial language a bit more problematic. As Neurath continues, "Whereas traditional language is overloaded with positive or negative judgments, a visual language eliminates judgment. Simplified pictures can convey information without bias, perhaps because they have been so little used for this purpose" (Ibid., 234). So, is it the intrinsic qualities of pictorial presentations as opposed to verbal ones that make them neutral and objective and less susceptible to manipulation? Or is it, on the other hand, their relatively short-lived use in modern times as means for manipulated communication of so-called knowledge claims? Right away, Neurath must find himself in a historically precarious position, when his insistence on the apolitical (negative and positive) character of his visual language can be challenged as being a language after all (open to multiple connotations, misinterpretations, and propagandistic manipulation). Though his intention of finding common visual ground, common visual language with which to transmit knowledge across national boundaries, seems to overcome previous uses of images that were bound by tradition, he may have opened himself to a political predicament even harsher than the one he wanted to overcome.

Assume, for a moment, that the public buys into the Neurath agenda for an international visual language (Isotype). Assume, as well, that the basis for this acceptance is that this language is indeed neutral, objective, and unbiased in any sense, namely, that it directly and explicitly represents the facts of the matter in the most simple and transparent way. If these assumptions were to be taken seriously, it would mean that the normal cognitive guard we assume when encountering any statement whatsoever would be completely absent, and therefore we'd be more open to accept as true whatever was transmitted to us. In fact, whatever implicit cues we normally deploy when reading anything (connotations, historical precedents, sarcasm, irony, and the like) would be eliminated. We'd simply accept it completely! And this is exactly when the scales can be tipped in the other direction—pretending that the facts are never disputed, but merely reported; pretending that knowledge is likewise never in flux, but permanent and absolute. And this, as history teaches us, is never the case.

By contrast to this view of visual communication, one that resonates with the current scientific-reductionist ideology of human nature as genetically determined, we can recall Nelson Goodman's concern with the languages of art. Following the lead of Ernest Gombrich, he admits that "there is no innocent eye," that "perception and interpretation are no separate operations; they are thoroughly interdependent" (Goodman 1976, 7–8). To use a specific example, he discusses the notion of perspective. As far as both Gombrich and Gibson claim, perspective isn't a "convention," but an appropriate representation of reality and its objects in space. But Goodman suggests by contrast that "pictures in perspective, like any others, have to be read; and the ability to read has to be acquired" (Ibid., 10–4). Moreover,

> The rules of pictorial perspective no more follow from the laws of optics than would rules calling for drawing the tracks parallel and the poles converging. In diametric contradiction to what Gibson says, the artist who wants to produce a spatial representation that the present-day Western eye will accept as faithful must defy the "laws of geometry" (Ibid., 16).

According to Goodman, then, there is no "independent standard of fidelity" (Ibid., 19) against which our representations must measure up, but instead there are ongoing conventionalized ways of seeing, ways by which we "translate" from the visual to the verbal, from reality out there to a drawing right here, from one age to another, and from one geographical location to another. In short, there are rules and cues, a visual syntax and a visual semantic matrix according to which communication is constructed. So, "if representing is a matter of classifying objects rather than imitating them," namely, organizing a set of data instead of assuming it's prefigured, "it is not a matter of passive reporting" (Ibid., 31). In these arguments and claims, Goodman follows the later Wittgenstein instead of the earlier one, that is, he's departing from the strict Vienna Circle claim to a direct, one-to-one representation of reality with statements (verbal or pictorial), and concedes the complex linguistic framework where humans interact and live, develop conventions and let a natural language evolve over time.

This view, incidentally, responds to some concerns in the philosophy of language. The Correspondence Theory of Truth, as it was eventually labeled, carried the day between the two World Wars and even later into the Anglo-American Analytic School as a way to remove linguistic and cultural biases and prejudices, confusions and puzzles. It was a method to achieve a universal, unified science underlying and clearly explaining all knowledge claims about nature. The beauty of the quest for universality and clarity, the kind of quest already advocated during the scientific revolutions of the seventeenth century, was not lost on those more interested in reaching social and political goals than on those concerned with epistemology and ontology. In the case of those pushing for social goals, the appeal to universality is an appeal to principles that transcend power relations, privilege, and tradition. It's an appeal for common ground on which to construct political institutions and develop social networks that are democratic and rational, accessible and mutable.

John Dewey, in this context, follows the trends of the Vienna Circle to simplify representation and communication of lived experiences. For him, too, there was a pragmatic agenda that drove him to reconsider art instrumentally, as a means to an end and not as an end in and of itself. Though not following the biological-reductionist view that human cognition is pre-wired identically (as we have seen above), he did want to break down the personal experiential encounters that human beings have with and in nature so as to familiarize themselves with a set of visual cues that could easily be used by others. According to Dewey, art mediates our experience of nature and therefore serves more effectively than words and language as a tool of communication and expression. The mediation is pragmatic in the sense that it performs a task or has a role we learn to appreciate over time, regardless of cultural differences.

But when we do so, suggests Ernst Gombrich, we have to take nature apart and then put it back together in a process that requires as much experimentation as observation. When doing so, we begin to appreciate that there is no innocent eye, no naïve observation. Whether we follow Norwood Hanson's dictum that all observations are "theory-laden" or follow Gombrich's insistence that our eyes are part of a complex cognitive process that has its own history and genealogy, we must concede that our representations are bound to be culturally informed. Anthropologists, such as Ian Jarvie, have demonstrated the ways in which members of cultures other than our own Western ones have a difficult time recognizing photographic images and those of the cinemas are if they were "realistic" depictions of nature and humans. The "others" had to learn to read these images since they were foreign to their context of observation.

As Nelson Goodman summarizes this line of argument, representing "is not a matter of copying but of conveying." Using the example of Renaissance perspective, he continues to say: "Pictures in perspective, like any others, have to be read; and the ability to read has to be acquired." In making his argument, Goodman reminds us to shed some of our western, technoscientific spectacles and realize that what has become in our minds a truly realistic, neutral, objective, and absolute representation of nature according to the laws of physics and optics is in fact only a convention we have come to accept.

For Goodman, then, representing is "a matter of classifying objects rather than of imitating them, of characterizing rather than of copying," so that the activity itself "is not a matter of passive reporting." Once the artist is understood to be an active participant, just as Stephen Toulmin acknowledges this in the case of scientist, then the act of representing can be understood as a creative endeavor. As such, artistic production is interpreting through and through, allowing cultural contexts to determine its scope and content, its style and distribution. The active participation of artists is determining what to represent and how to represent it and thus allows for cultural, political, and social fluctuation even within the same period of time. Cultural relativism and the differences among artists, then, undermine the possibility of universalizing artistic products, not to mention the quest for universal perception by different viewers.

If we read works of art in line with our intuitional pedagogy and the ideological restrictions of our political leadership, then it would make sense that the community of artists would be the target of those trying to influence the general public. This might be the case within fascist regimes or within contemporary hyper-capitalism. In both cases the propaganda machines could make use of visual images to encourage, discourage, entreat, threaten, and influence how people perceive themselves and their surroundings. It's no wonder that when the Nazis marched into Vienna, one of their first targets was Neurath's museum. What better use of seemingly universal symbols to promote Social Nationalism? This deep appreciation for the power of images also informed Stalin in commissioning artists to produce large murals and oversized sculptures, while exiling all dissidents to the gulags of Siberia.

Following Goodman's view, we find statements, such as "Nature is a product of art and discourse" (Ibid., 33), that must give us pause if the political dimension comes into play. So, the "facts" and "knowledge" as Neurath described them aren't the solid, undisputed foundations upon which we build our decisions in a democracy. Rather, they are produced, constructed, invented, if you wish, so that all of a sudden it matters who does the producing, constructing, and inventing. Do they have room for manipulation? Yes. Can they enhance a claim or forward a political agenda based on whatever they take to be the knowledge of the day? Yes. How can their claims be assessed or criticized? What "independent" standards can be appealed to? You see, the quest for a uniform, universal means of communication that adheres to a uniform, universal reality that is understood in uniform, universal ways is not unreasonable—in fact, it seems desirable!

III: THE BAUHAUS'S DREAM OF UNIVERSAL ACCESS

As Andreas Haus reminds us, the establishment of the Bauhaus was predicated on previous attempts to respond to two major concerns in the unified Germany of the late nineteenth century and early twentieth century.

On the one hand, the Weimar Republic was concerned with providing sufficient economic stimulus and hope to its citizens, and on the other, the devastation and eventual effects of the first World War were of concern to the refined sensibilities and romantic aspirations of European culture. The German *Werkbund* (Art and Craft League) of 1907 brought together architects and artists, art historians and industrialists in order to promote a cultural setting with specific economic goals: "The aim of the Bund is to ennoble craft work by combining arts, industry and crafts through education, propaganda and a united front on the issues involved" (Fiedler and Feierabend 1999, 16). As we can tell from the expressed concerns and agenda of the Bund, propaganda isn't the sole purview of politicians, but runs deep through any organization that has goals or wishes to promote specific results based on specific ideas.

Similar to the goals of the German *Werkbund*, the *Arbeitsrat fur Kunst* (Working Council for Art) of 1918 followed the establishment of soldiers' and workers' councils dedicated to bring functionalism into the lofty echelons of art schools and art councils. In their literature, they suggested that "The old state ruled autocratically over art. The new state must first serve in oder to acquire the lofty epithet 'free'" (Ibid., 17). With this background in mind, and with his own involvement in these movements, Walter Gropius was in a good position to establish the Bauhaus. As Haus insists, the emphasis was "not so much the products to be created as the social and spiritual community of the creators" (Ibid., 18). Obviously, one can detect different strands in the movement and in its practices, from utopian visions to pedagogical reforms, from romantic zeal to return to the folklike crafts and to the hyper-commercialized developments of the industrial revolution. But regardless of how one views the details of the movement that lasted officially from 1919 to 1933, it's clear that it had an immense impact on national debates in Germany and on the international community (see illustrations 26–29 that show a spectrum of abstract images from Germany, United States, Italy, and the Soviet Union of the same period).

The guiding principles of the Bauhaus could be understood as having a foundation that is universal in its appeal: combining functionalism with aesthetic simplicity, eschewing the wasteful (criminal, in Loos's opinion) frills of the aristocracy and elevating the social or aesthetic status of the actual practices of artisans who produce useful tools and products for the marketplace (see illustration 22 of the Bauhaus's chair and how it fits into the visual model of the Isotype). There is no reason to waste time and money on elaborate facades for buildings, especially when a nation is trying to house the soldiers coming home from the front as well as trying to fill orders in factories that must be economically viable. Before long, the ideology of a nascent democracy was intertwined with its industrial and economic conditions, so that the notions of freedom and opportunity, success and progress had to be accounted for outside academic circles. Within this environment, the Bauhaus could flourish and set the tone for the future. But just as much as it had its national appeal, as a Germanic attempt to overcome the past and prepare for the future, it also had an appeal outside these national borders. It's therefore not surprising that when the National Socialist party came into power, the Bauhaus and its agenda came under scrutiny and eventually were suspended and closed.

Peter Hahn, in pulling together archival materials of the Bauhaus movement, explains the conditions under which the Dessau facility of the Bauhaus was closed, especially in light of the rise of National Socialism. Just as the original director, Gropius, was concerned with the political climate of the Weimer Republic ethos of rebuilding Germany after World War I, trying to bridge art and technology, aesthetics and design, so was the last director, Mies van der Rohe, embroiled in the rise of the political power of National Socialism. Was the Bauhaus movement "German" enough? Was it too communist or socialist in character, given the pedagogical principles of the school and its commitment to workshops and social progress?

> Today it seems astonishing that members of the National Socialist "*Kampfbund*" should have even given the Bauhaus a second thought. There were at that time, however, numerous efforts among National Socialist cultural politicians to promote modern art and architecture and Expressionism, as "German" currents, to the status of national art. It wasn't until 1934 that the Nazis finally condemned modern art as fundamentally "un-German," "alien," and "Bolshevist" (Hahn 2002, 230).

There was always a socialist or communist element in the Bauhaus, at least in the sense that it was also to be found in Neurath's Isotype method. If their ideas worked at all, if they made any sense, then they could work or make sense to anyone anywhere—indeed, there is a national past that can be appealed to in order to set in motion the future; but that past could be any "national" past, any folklike practice or tradition, and not a specific German or British or Russian one. This, as the quote above indicates, was too vague and broad to satisfy the officials of the National Socialist party, for they wanted an Aryan uniqueness and supremacy, and not just any kind of background.

What we wish to emphasize at this juncture, without elaborating on the details of the Bauhaus movement and its practices, is that any claim for universality has a political or ideological component to it that is open to artistic manipulation. It's not only the case that art can be at the service of propaganda; that much is fairly common knowledge now, and requires little debate. But that one can look backward, so to speak, at any aesthetic expression and find in it a specific ideological statement or conviction is a bit more controversial. This is true if one believes that symbols and images are "read" and interpreted within a cultural context since they are opaque and loaded with meanings and connotations, as opposed to believing that they are transparent and universally recognizable. It's easy, then, to decide how to appreciate the political dimension of artworks and the political position that the artistic community holds in a society.

IV: DO NATIONAL IDENTITIES LOOK ALIKE?

The positions artists hold in a society depend also on what specific medium they are using. Unless one is labeled "degenerate," in the Nazi sense of degenerate art, one can continue to perform their tasks without much wrath of the authorities; one can hide, so to speak. But this could mean a variety of things. For example, how do we approach diverse groups of artists, such as architects (Bauhaus movement), musicians (Schoenberg's atonality), and contemporary digital art (computers) where technology itself is considered to transcend national borders? Are artists then claiming to use technology in the service of their political "masters," whether they are democratic capitalists who promote the advertisement of products in the marketplace or fascist dictators who promote the notion of freedom through hard labor and dedication to the national spirit? On some level, of course, artists are complicit in the actions of the political domain, whether they'd like to admit to it or not. On another level, the very use of their tools could be considered bourgeois or progressive, folkish or international. Whatever their choice, the ideological framework doesn't disappear, it only recedes to the background, where claims are made for objectivity and truth, accuracy and universality of all knowledge production machines in the age of globalization.

Without conceding to an extreme view of cultural relativism, we must recognize the differences in cultural perception and reception of visual images. Does this negate the utopian quest for universal spirituality and redemption (under the title of the sublime)? Or does this open the possibility of a universal appeal with national and cultural variations? Can art be produced in a fashion and with an appeal that transcends national boundaries without losing its authenticity? Does a universal pretense necessitate domination and suppression?

Perhaps we tend to be more forgiving toward the choices artists make when faced with their predicament because we believe that the techno-scientific world (from tools to telecommunication) is itself political. It is political in terms of power relations within sovereign states, the dominance of money over cultural productions, and the concentration of economic and political power in the hands of the few. So, the very pretense of artistic (cultural) neutrality and purity evaporates before our eyes. Perhaps the next question should be: If purity is an artistic impossibility, can spirituality save the souls of artists? And if the answer is yes, do we mean by spirituality so-called folk art, religious experiences, a sense of the Kantian Sublime, or the integrity of individual artists?

Neurath, for one, was concerned that the most important elements of our visual perception will be grasped immediately and that this would be true for everyone. He understood that layers of meanings could be added to our visual experience, and therefore he sought to strip it to its bare essentials, as he construed them. He aimed, to put it briefly, to engage that fundamental element of our visual and cognitive perception so as to be able to transmit information to anyone anywhere in the world. This may sound odd, but consider for a moment that when crossing linguistic boundaries, as in the contemporary push toward economic globalization, we find it comforting to know that certain instructions and warnings will be pictorial rather than verbal. For example, wheelchair accessibility or nonsmoking areas are labeled in airports and public places pictorially in a manner that seems clear to anyone regardless of their language of origin. There should be no excuse, so the reasoning goes, for anyone not to know what's going on here, even if you happen to be thousands of miles away from your hometown.

This reductionist move, as we saw already, though appealing on the face of it, is highly problematic, if not downright mistaken. But, in defense of Neurath's work, we should recall the strong reductionist convictions of the Vienna Circle in general and the linguistic moves undertaken in that period in particular. Their convictions were also informed and propelled by technoscientific developments that alluded to the objectivity, value-neutrality, and universality of our knowledge production machines in the modern age of bureaucratization. The universal language of nature was understood to be divine at one point, Latin at another, and mathematical at yet another point in time. What's wrong with designating this universal language of nature and epistemology pictorial?

The power of the image was already known to religious leaders some five thousands years ago. The Jews maintained a Biblical injunction against the creation of "graven images" of God, while the Catholics were deliberate in magnifying images of the crucifix, Mary, and all the saints. As much as the Jews feared debasing the "unseeable," the Catholics dominated the visual world and the history of art in the Western world. To some extent, religious institutions appreciated the universalizing aspects of the visual world, and decided to appropriate them in their own respective ways. The missionary zeal of the Catholic Church could benefit from setting up images accessible to all, transcending, as they were, cultural boundaries, appealing to all of humanity, and invoking awe in those who behold them. Is the image of Christ on the cross universal? Does it bespeak of human suffering, repentance, and redemption? Can anyone "misread" the image or read into it something completely un-Christian?

Without belaboring these questions, we would like to add to this set of arguments. In favor of the potential for universal appeal of visual representation is the notion of the sublime. Aesthetic experiences, whether conceptualized in Kant's sense of the *Third Critique* or in the senses dating back to Socrates or those extending to the present, have been described in terms of the sublime. The sublime is unspeakable, as Lyotard claims, or universal, as Kant claims. The sublime is the moment in human experience when words fail to describe that which is seen and felt, that which is experienced and accepted. It is a moment that repeats itself whether we observe a natural phenomenon or are standing in front of a painting in a climate-controlled museum. But is it universal? And if it is, what does it mean for it to be universal? Is it universal because repeatable or because it evokes a common reaction or response in all people across cultural boundaries? Is the museum setting itself not unique enough to deter, rather than invite, all viewers? And what about those engaged in the production and distribution of aesthetic experiences, those dedicating their lives to creating artworks and displaying them for public consumption?

While there are artists and art movements intent on promoting certain ideas and ideals, as can be seen in propaganda-like artworks, there are artists and art movements intent on having a universal appeal. Perhaps this is the intent of some artists who believe that the encounter with an abstract piece of art is an expression of the sublime or can bring about an experience of the sublime. One could examine the lessons artists have learned in the twentieth century in regard to the political context in which they had to work, so as to appreciate their predicament in the present century. But, can an appeal to abstract art transcend national boundaries even though it has specific patriotic and ideological messages in terms of how the sublime is defined? We can admit that just as there is a potential for universal appeal within nationalist artworks, so there is a potential for nationalist appeal in what might seem, on the face of it, universally appealing art. Isn't Sherrie Levine's gold-coated urinal that pays homage to Duchamp's *Ready-Mades* not a capitalist, western European, and Americanized way of mocking the bourgeois art establishment? Is this cynical commentary of any appeal to Asian, African, and Russian audiences? What meaning does a urinal as artwork have to those who don't enjoy indoor plumbing and electricity?

Perhaps we tend to be more forgiving toward the choices artists make when faced with their respective predicaments because the technoscientific world (from tools to telecommunication) is itself political. It is political in terms of power relations within sovereign states, the dominance of money over cultural productions, and the concentration of economic and political power in the hands of the few. So, the very pretense of artistic (cultural) neutrality and purity, at least in the sense of universality, evaporates before our eyes. Perhaps this is a good point to switch to the set of arguments and examples that suggest the inherent impossibility of universal appeal in and of artworks, so that every artistic production is bound by its context and a set of interpretations that define it.

Without conceding to an extreme view of cultural relativism, we must recognize the differences in cultural perception and reception of visual images. Does this recognition negate the utopian quest for universal spirituality and redemption (under the title of the sublime)? Or does this open the possibility of a universal appeal with national and cultural variations? Can art be produced in a fashion and with an appeal that transcends national boundaries without losing its authenticity? Does a universal pretense necessitate domination and suppression?

Without answering all of these questions, some admittedly rhetorical, let us finish here with a few comments so as to set up the next chapter. The ideology and politics of fascism claimed no national boundaries in their artistic appeal, and therefore thought of themselves in universal terms, no different from the terms democracy thinks of as its principles and practices. There was a sense in which what was true for Hitler or Stalin or Mussolini should have been true for everyone. It's the "everyone" that is here under scrutiny. It is one thing to appeal to one's national compatriots under a patriotic flag and slogans that exclude others in order to ensure domestic cohesion, and quite another to appeal to the membership of one's species. But to think that this difference will be resolved through and by the artistic community is to miss the point. For no matter how powerful and wealthy their world becomes, no matter how global its financial reach in networks of distribution and promotion, it will always remain part of the nation-states and the industrial-military complex that subsidizes it. Unless the art world becomes autonomous, there is no way for it to make an appeal of universality in an oppressed and greedy environment, in an environment that consumes itself with its own consumption. In thinking about these questions of politics and ideology when it comes to art, we can recall the Bauhaus as a case in point: Would its eventual success and universal appeal have turned it into a global, corporate medusa whose tentacles could not be avoided? Is the antidote to nationalism capitalism? But isn't capitalism an ideology of its own, no matter how popular or despised it might be here or there?

These questions set the stage for the next chapter in which we reexamine the role of the artistic community in constructing national monuments and establishing pedagogical institutions to train and initiate its recruits to further the aesthetic experience of the public at large.

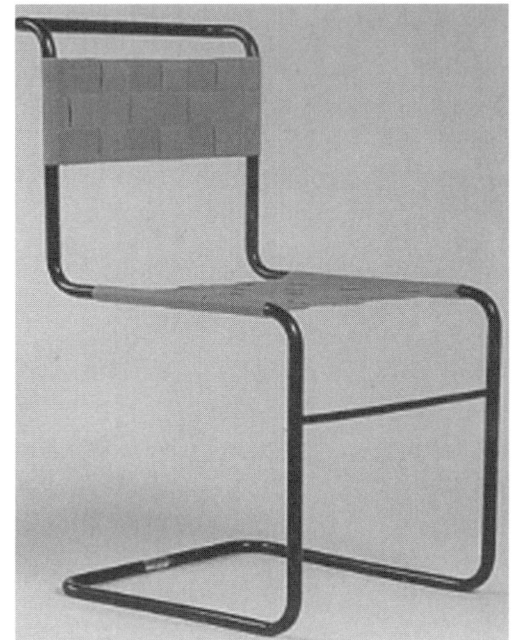

22

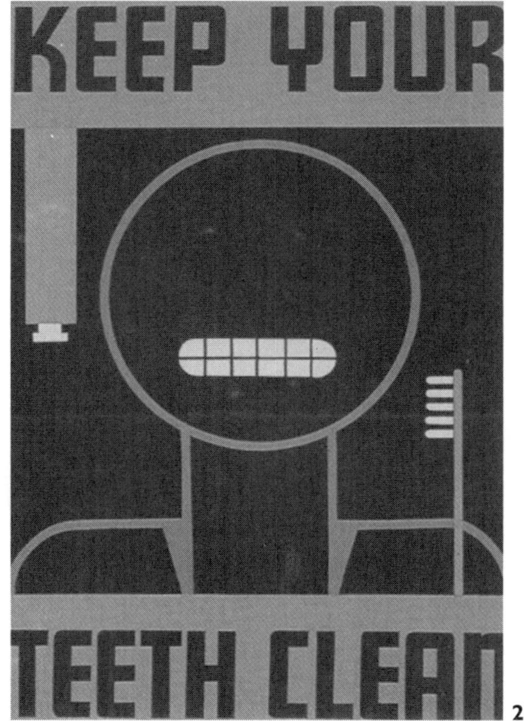

23

24

25

STAATLICHES BAUHAUS
AUSSTELLUNG
JULI SEPT
WEIMAR
1923

26

КЛИНОМ
КРАСНЫМ
БЕЙ
БЕЛЫХ

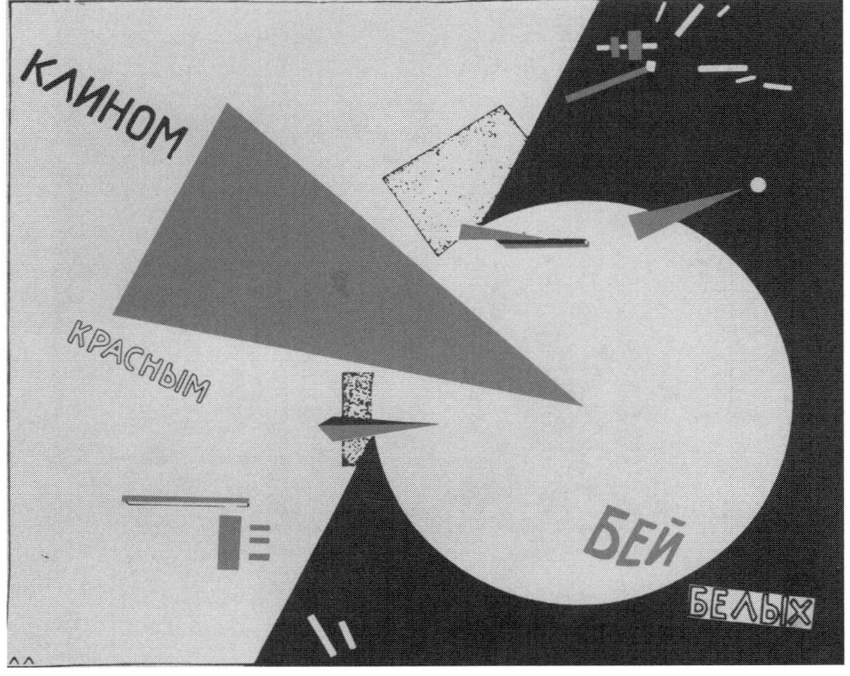

27

Vizzoli
ITALIANI
(OMAGGIO) ARTI GRAFICHE NAVARRA S.A. MILANO
PROPAGANDA "Maga"

28

POSTERS and ART PROCESSES
METHODS MATERIALS TOOLS:
POSTERS · GRAPHIC ART
FRESCO AND SCULPTURE
EXHIBITION
FEDERAL ART GALLERY
225 WEST 57 STREET N.Y.C
DECEMBER 1 TO 18 1937
10 TO 4 WEEKDAYS 12 TO 5 SATURDAYS
FEDERAL ART PROJECT
WORKS PROGRESS ADMINISTRATION

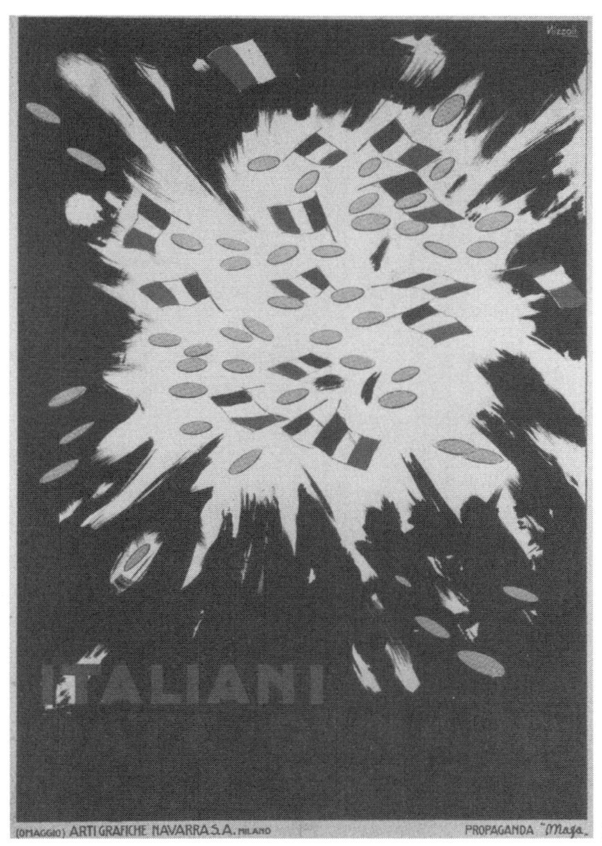

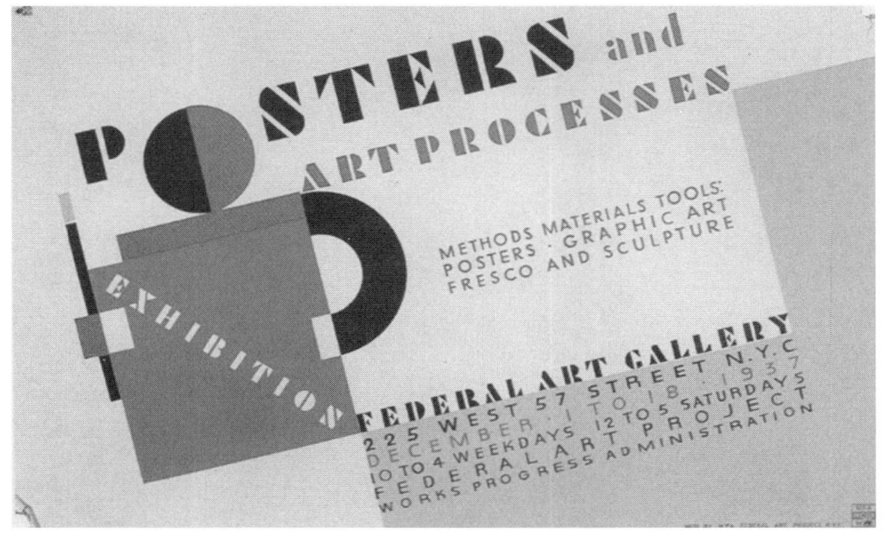

29

4

THE PEDAGOGICAL PREDICAMENT

I: IN SEARCH OF A MIDDLE GROUND

In this chapter we revisit the issues raised in the previous chapter, but with an interesting twist. Instead of revisiting the predicament facing artists who try to embody their products with national identity while appealing to international cues and tastes, we suggest two areas where this predicament is apparent. One area is the way we erect monuments that depict heroic gestures during battles and wars and that help commemorate the past; the other area is the way we educate artists in the making, the way we indoctrinate them into our national identity while inspiring them to communicate with the world at large. In both cases, there are problems inherent in the role the artistic community plays in our social and political arena; at the same time, these problems can suggest some ways in which we can confront and propose solutions to them.

Most of our national monuments that commemorate wars or national heroes use "realistic" depictions: soldiers in a battle scene, Lincoln seated in an oversized chair, even the *Statute of Liberty* (with its allegorical French influences). Memories, though, are more "idealistic" and in this sense more abstract. We recall the scene, but perhaps not all its details; we recall the event, but not all those who participated in it. At times our "forgetfulness" is deliberate, and in this sense selective (at times racist and discriminatory as in the case of the Civil War). Can we ask what *Mount Rushmore*, a national monument many consider expressing a program of memorializing the expansion of the American Republic, the work of an artist consumed with the fantasy of Western "rugged individualism" and constructed in an area considered sacred to its native people might mean to contemporary Native Americans? To some extent, everyone believes that the simple principles of democracy, relying primarily on the principles of freedom and equality, progress and personal hard work, need no further explanation—they are, as the American Constitution claims, "self evident." Be that as it may, we suggest that the specific American variant of democracy that evolved over the past two centuries has presented itself in images in particular ways, covering some principles and areas of emphasis that have a national character of their own (for example, allowing slavery until the Civil War and denying suffrage to women until 1920). And for some, these images and myths, ways of representing democracy, are a bit more problematic: "and this (*The Mount Rushmore Memorial*) is what conquering means. They could just as well have carved this mountain into a huge cavalry boot standing on a dead Indian" (Lame Deer, Sioux medicine man, in Boime 1991, 166; see illustrations 14 and 15).

In what follows we'd like to suggest that despite the public desire for realistic depictions of memorials, it's more useful and honest to have an abstract piece of art as a memorial. Put differently, though it may sound paradoxical, abstract, opaque commemoration is a more effective way to elicit emotional reaction and bring to life the past than a realistic, transparent one. Perhaps this is because of our "natural disposition," as discussed by those tracing our perception to a genetic basis. If we follow this line of argument, then, one could accommodate multiple perspectives of the recollection of the past and produce so-called universal if not uniform, emotional responses that transcend the limitations of a realistic depiction. A parallel argument that runs through our discussion relates to the appeal of abstract, universal art as transcending national boundaries. The questions raised here also deal with the concern with recalling the specifics of the tragedies of our past or evoking in the present an emotional response to forge patriotism, nationalism, or a healing process in the viewers.

II: ABSTRACT MEMORIES: RECALLING REALITY

To remember something is to bring it to life, once again, in the present. Since we are not dealing here with the psychological aspects of such an undertaking nor with all its related social-historical aspects, we'll limit our discussion to the art world and its various depictions of the past. However focused our attention is on the art world, we are aware of the influences from related fields on the manner in which artists may be engaged in the creation of artworks depicting the past. We'll briefly spell out how this translates from the scientific and the legal arenas into the art world.

In the scientific world there has been a long-running debate about the status of empirical evidence in substantiating claims about reality. Ever since the scientific revolutions of the seventeenth century, the empiricists—those committed to the verification of empirical claims through observations—and the rationalists—those who distrust observations as either prone to errors or theory-laden—have been debating the merits of their respective methods of inquiry. What was at stake for them was the eventual credibility and legitimacy of the scientific claims about nature, the world, or human behavior. What seems trivial and transparent from one perspective, say, the fact that the sun rises every morning from the east, has been contested by some because of the theoretical framework within which such a statement of fact makes sense or can be verified, confirmed, or falsified. In short, the evidence one brings from the field, so-called, is itself contested. Besides, as Hume has eloquently complained, just because something has been repeatedly observed in the past does not mean that on sound logical grounds we can assume it to be observed in the future. This, incidentally, is called the problem of induction. It was partially resolved much later by Karl Popper, who suggested that we count as certain only those instances when something is proved to be in error, mistaken, or false right here and now and not render our speculation about the future to be scientific at all (unless refutable in principle, and hopefully in practice). Now, we digress into the world of scientific methodology in order to glean some of its concerns and insights as they relate to the problematic situation of basing our judgment in the present on evidence from the past.

In a similar manner, we wish to briefly digress into the legal world, where questions of evidence and testimony loom large over any judgment whatsoever. Should we consider the testimony of everyone as being on equal footing? Can we separate, as the Aristotelian logicians beseeched us some two thousand years ago, between the statement and the one who is making it? The *ad hominem* quandary in courts of law is usually resolved illogically: we ask for character witnesses in order to bolster the credibility of the witness. We thereby refuse to adhere to the logicians' plea to separate the message from the messenger, so to speak, and thereby believe that the testimony of a respectable person is closer to the truth of the matter than that of a homeless person or a person with a criminal record. But the facts should be substantiated by the evidence at hand regardless of who is testifying! In addition to this quandary, there is another set of issues that relate to the kind of evidence considered relevant or significant in court cases. We have different criteria of truth and certainty when we render judgment today about something that happened in the past: Must we know beyond the shadow of doubt? Or is reasonable certainty enough? Is circumstantial evidence sufficient to convict? These are questions that are answered differently in different cases depending on the severity of the crime and the criteria for conviction imposed by the law. Just as in the case of the scientific world, the legal world can shed some light on some of the issues plaguing those concerned with recollections and the appropriate manner in which they ought to be expressed and represented in the present.

So, back to the art world and its attempts to memorialize or provide testimonials about past occurrences, whether tragic or nostalgic. Since the very activity of re-presentation is philosophically problematic and aesthetically challenging, an artist must acknowledge a fundamental truth: an artwork is by definition incomplete, misleading, under-determined, biased, selective, and manipulative. The creative process itself is informed by the individual artist selectively choosing the subject matter, the materials, and the format with which to express an idea, image, or emotion. The process of selection is understood to express the biases of the artist, the particular perspective from which the choice is being made. Old-fashioned Renaissance-influenced three-dimensional linear perspective drawings and paintings were supposed to portray an Archimedean vantage point, a bird's-eye view of the world from nowhere or God's sanctuary. By the twentieth century, the claims for objectivity and value-neutrality had been expunged from the intellectual domain to be replaced with a greater self-reflexivity in all domains of research and activity. We have realized that we bring our own prejudices into our work; we read into texts our own concerns; we create images that are partially our own internal ones and only partially those of the external world. To some extent the art world has agreed with this situation, since works of art bear their creators' signature—it's your work, your ideas put on display! With a stroke of one's pen, so to speak, a piece of art has been identified with its creator, has been linked to a particular person, rather than to a disembodied, machine-generating entity.

We'd like to suggest, then, that the naïve view of *mimesis* as the process of copying or mimicking that which is "out there" doesn't exist in principle, and is undertaken only as an aesthetic assertion (that is, pedagogically informed). Even in the cases of photography, the original expectation of a one-to-one correspondence between the object and its image has been shattered quickly. The choice of equipment and materials, the choice of an angle and lighting, the choice of developing techniques, and the context within which the image is chosen—all of these betray a deliberate (if at times subconscious) decision on the part of artists; theirs is therefore a process of selection, where preferences are made clear to viewers post hoc. One could extend our discussion into architecture, dance, and music, since we consider them exciting parallels reflecting the same process of deliberate selection.

Even when we agree that artists as creative agents of their culture are participating in a selective process, their product can take on different forms of presentation. In order to refocus our discussion of memories, monuments, and commemorative projects, we'd like to suggest two stylistic or formal categories that dominate these kind of artworks: realist and abstract. In what follows, we'll discuss the characteristics of each format.

First, realistic depictions. To some extent, realistic depictions have the pretense of being immediate, transparent, clearly defined, and objective. The general public assumes that photojournalism is a form of capturing the moment on film and then reproducing it for mass consumption. The idea behind it, and one that is reinforced anytime a television camera crew goes to the "scene," is that what is seen is the real thing without any interference by the camera crew or the photographer.

Think for a moment of one of the most famous Vietnam era photographs to hit print media and provoke the American public—an image is worth a thousand words (for example, the execution of the captured Viet Cong man at point-blank range).

Likewise, sculptures of great leaders, whether we think of the *Lincoln Memorial* or any of the Soviet statues of Stalin (see illustrations 12 and 13), seem to capture an expression, a posture that is particularly germane to the hero in question. Though the settings may have broader connotations—horseback riding, seated at an oversized chair, leading troops—the individual in question is presumed to be depicted as realistically as possible, with as much attention to detail as possible. Of course, there are other monuments, such as the *Statue of Liberty*, where realistic depiction is subservient to the ideals in question, such as liberty, strength, hope, and dreams (with their respective French influences).

But as hard as they all try, as realistic as they all seem to be, and as much as they all attempt to capture the past in a way that would appeal to and make sense in the present, we claim that such realistic depictions and representations are in fact less effective on a personal level. They are less effective, perhaps even a bit detached, because they depict the "other" in its fullest sense and thereby set up an alienating distance that undermines personal identification. The other is in this overdetermined posture that leaves little for the imagination, and the invitation to gaze becomes an invitation to admire. The invitation to admire then reflects back on the viewer and may inspire either awe or resentment, but it definitely opens a separating gulf.

What is the case with commemorative monuments? Whether we think of those holding the flag in Iwo Jima . . . or the firefighters depicted in the wake of 9/11 . . . or the alternative Vietnam Veterans' Memorial in Washington, DC, which represent naturalistic soldiers and healers, in all cases the images are complete, and they tell a full story (see illustrations 30 and 31). In their depictions and the care with which natural or realistic details are represented, they seem to leave little for the imagination. They contain or express, in Edward Wyatt's words, "stark realism" that embodies convincing evidence of what had happened. The emotional impact is direct and immediate, like the architectural design or the photograph in the print media. There is a sense in which a naturalistic depiction is equated with telling a narrative as completely as possible, as if retelling the horrors and sorrows undergone by those who suffered or perished in a catastrophic event. Incidentally, this is what Steven Spielberg intended to do in the opening scene of *Saving Private Ryan* with excruciating and gory detail.

But perhaps what is at stake in remembering an event or retelling the past is not a re-presentation or the appeal to an emotional reaction, but a form of healing, laying to rest that trauma that took place in the past and is brought to a closure in the present act of viewing. As Paul Goldberg argues in the case of commemorating the attack on the World Trade Center on September 11, 2001:

> The monument issue is complicated by a tendency in the last few years to think of public memorials as "healing" places for families. But great memorials also inspire awe, and make it possible to transcend the simply personal meaning of an event. The best way to deal with a memorial is probably to have an international design competition—it takes time. . . . The metaphors that make for powerful memorials tend to be clearer when the immediate experiences of a catastrophic event recedes. (95)

So, perhaps the distance-effects of time play a role in the depiction and viewing of memorials. And perhaps what becomes clear in time, as Goldberg says, is not the event itself, but our own emotional reactions, our own ways of conceptualizing what happened, and our ways of processing the emotional residues left behind. This way of thinking brings us closer to the second alternative mode of representing the past, abstract depictions.

As we have seen in the previous chapter, Otto Neurath developed in the early part of the twentieth century the International System of TYpographic Picture Education, which allowed for a visual representation of data in formalistic, abstract, and minimalist fashion. To recall, the international appeal of the museum because of its claim for immediate comprehension by literate and illiterate viewers alike made it one of the first targets of the invading Nazis when they entered Vienna in 1939. They clearly understood the propagandist power of such visual imaging, and therefore wanted to use the technique for their own ideological purposes. Illiterates could identify with the images and be impressed by whatever message was transmitted through them. The potential for personalizing past experiences and exposures gives abstract rendering the power and visual advantage over naturalistic representation.

From this perspective, then, we suggest that the psychological appeal, even if not fully emotional in the psychoanalytic sense of revealing the subconscious, is individualistic and requires a deeper level of engagement. In order to comprehend the image, such as Maya Lin's memorial to the Vietnam War's soldiers, in order to make it your own, you are forced to reflect on something other than the object before you. The object itself, the black wall and the engraved names on it, as opposed the naturalistic alternative shown before, opens the door to a path your mind must take, and wherever your mind takes you, it is your own journey, cognitive and emotive, but thoroughly personal (see illustration 32).

What we suggest here is the paradoxical condition for personal engagement in the face of commemorative memorials—the more abstract, the better. The more removed from the actual depiction of the actual trauma, the more real and personal. As such, less realism in the monument will enable a more accurate re-presentation of the disaster or trauma being depicted. We know people died, and we mourn their innocent deaths. But in order to honor their memory, in order to dignify the horrible death they endured, we should tread gently and softly with images that show respect, that let us reflect on them and on us at the same time.

Instead of leaving the impression that there is a clear-cut aesthetic advantage to abstract art over more naturalistic images, let's observe a case where the lines of demarcation between the two are blurred. An example could be Maya Lin's wall, because the very names engraved on the black slab are real in the sense of being identified with real people. So, the sense of realism itself is being challenged here. Another example could be the chairs at the Oklahoma City bombing's memorial site (see illustration 33), since they serve both as realistic reminders of empty chairs where people once sat, and at the same time their sculptural texture and design are quite abstract. A third case in point would be the room at the Holocaust Memorial Museum in Washington, DC, that is filled with shoes found at the Majdanek death camp. The shoes are as real as they come, but seeing an enormous pile of them brings up the memory of those who once wore them and who were gassed to their death by the Nazis. So, there is no simple answer to the question about the most appropriate and effective way to commemorate the horrors of the past.

III: SANCTIFYING A NATIONAL IDENTITY: AUTHENTICITY

Folk art is understood as a repository of traditional values that have lasted the test of time. In contemporary culture there are the pressures to preserve folk art as one of the only genuine regional and national expressions of a culture, while at the same there are counterpressures to commercialize folk art and appropriate it for international tourism (as an attempt to universalize its images and message). This tendency to embrace and the pressure to exploit such claims for authenticity can be seen with Picasso's use in the visual arts, Bartok in music, and even Pueblo Indian arts and crafts. Authenticity lies not in a commitment to a stylistic direction but to an embrace of folk tradition as the source where the authentic character of a national identity is revealed. The underlying theme here is the parallel tendency to try to make folk art appeal universally, while retaining its authenticity.

Another way of approaching the issues that interest us in terms of the predicament that underlies any attempt to retain an authentic and personal voice while appealing to a wide audience is by focusing on different aesthetic genres, one of them being Southwestern art. Southwestern art, if there is such a category in art history, connotes certain images and ideological commitments. For example, one thinks of vast landscapes and limitless horizons (as originally portrayed by the "sublime painters" in the nineteenth century), of indigenous cultures (from Native Americans to coyotes), folklore and crafts, in short, the exotic "others" not included in the urban, industrial centers. But, of course, Southwestern art is a fabrication, often to elevate the status and a way to promote borderline "kitch" art that plays into the economic interests of gallery owners and potential art collectors and poster consumers.

Yet, instead of dismissing Southwestern art offhand, we'd like to distill some elements of this genre that might retain an aesthetic appeal and credibility. Instead of following any art critics in describing and analyzing Southwestern art in terms of modernist criteria or classic art history genealogy, we'd like to suggest that this way of finding merit in popular culture and art isn't a condescending way for connoisseurs to elevate folklore art, but rather an acknowledgment of the open-ended art appreciation and engagement that defy establishment judgments and interpretations. From our perspective, the aesthetic gatekeepers should invite as many genres and artists to create whatever work they wish so that any aesthetic experience can become self-legitimating.

For us, a self-legitimating art production contains all the standard elements taught in art schools and institutions, such as form, style, color, historical fit, coherence, defiance, critical engagement with other artists, and the like, as well as the deliberate and self-conscious attempt to reject these said criteria and refuse to fully participate in the strictures of the artistic community. This is not to say that only avant-garde artists or those claiming to be outside the "establishment" are bona fide artists; rather, it's a way to highlight the predicament of artists wishing to be both "inside" and "outside" of their community, critically engaged and yet refusing to respond to the aesthetic terms already prefigured for them by others.

In some peculiar way, there are interesting parallels between the reception and acceptance/rejection of Norman Rockwell's work (see illustration 34) and those of Southwestern artists because in both cases they represent an antimodernist approach to art (see illustration 35). They draw on native folk art, on images that are common and unpretentious, seemingly naturalistic in a naïve-realist sense. But as hard as they attempt to immerse their work in localized, regional traditions and customs, they also offer an aesthetic experience that has a universal appeal. In doing so, we ask ourselves, are they imposing the kind of artistic criteria of universal or categorical standards that are similar to those imposed under modernist genres or fascist regimes? We know that this question sounds preposterous, but what it implies or uncovers is the predicament of aesthetic appeal that interests us: Can there be a universal standard for beauty, or is it by definition historically and culturally constructed? Though we recalled earlier our appreciation of Noam Chomsky's theoretical and experimental work in regard to deep grammatical structures wired into the human brain, we still remain skeptical when such arguments are applied to cultural critiques and expressions as found in the artistic community. Moreover, we believe that the leaders who promote ideological convictions find good allies among artists who are willing to represent to the community at large the ideas and ideals of certain political agendas. It is in this sense, once again, that we discover the predicament of artists whose authenticity can be manipulated either inadvertently or with full complicity.

So, is Norman Rockwell a commercial artist who can be dismissed as a lackey for the reigning ideology of family values, Thanksgiving dinner, and even the significance of the New England Protestant work ethic? Likewise, should we dismiss Southwestern art and Pueblo Indians who produce arts and crafts for tourists as nothing but representing the frontier, rugged individualism, self-sufficiency, and even entrepreneurship, the kind of antiurban images that inspire Americans (from urban settings) to pursue manifest destiny of conquest and wealth? We raise these questions not necessarily as condemnation of the kind of works produced within these genres, but rather as an illustration of how so-called authentic, naturalistic, naïve-realist, pastoral, and folksy art can become commercialized and therefore less local, regional, and authentic.

The predicament of authenticity can be viewed on three parallel levels: first, in terms of local versus universal aesthetic appeal; second, in terms of the compromises made in the very production of the artworks; and third, in terms of the accommodation to commercial pressures. Is Southwestern art produced with industrial items provided originally by traders and colonializing Eurocentrist cowboys identical in its authentic claims to those pieces produced with indigenous resources? Are woven tapestries produced with sheep or horsehair raised in the pueblos as authentic as those produced with industrial materials shipped weekly from urban centers? And what about the commercial success they are enjoying today? Have any of their colors and patterns been scaled to meet consumers' tastes? Have any sales deadlines demanded mass production and western-style quality controls?

Likewise, has Rockwell's enormous commercial success as an illustrator and magazine-cover artist whose work is mass produced and reproduced been the reason why he has been dismissed for decades as not being a serious fine artist? Has he been the mouthpiece for political agendas or has he been able to maintain his artistic autonomy? There is something about his work that is charming enough to seduce the critic, not to mention the collector and museum viewer. His appeal is to a wide audience that has taken his message for granted, accepted the underlying ideology almost without suspicion. In this sense, then, how different is he from the Fascist propagandist who delivers the political message without remorse or second thoughts? Is Rockwell therefore complicit in defending and perpetuating the hegemony of white, middle-class, Eurocentrist nuclear families? Yet, even when all of these questions are answered in the affirmative, there is something unmistakenly American about his work; something we all recognize as wholesome and real: this is how American farmers and factory workers really look and act! This is indeed our American dream! (See illustrations 36 and 37 of two Rockwell images from his "democratic process" series.)

The issue that bothers us is the quest for authenticity in the name of national identity based on tradition and cultural commitments while not realizing the extent to which this very quest is universal and seeks universal legitimation. Put differently, can one retain a personal aesthetic (Rockwell) and indigenous authenticity (Indian Pueblo arts and crafts) in the midst of a global culture, that is, a culture that transcends the traditional boundaries of borders and languages? American products, such as Levis jeans and Coca-Cola, have an appeal or repulsion effect anywhere in the world. Certain musical genres are heard on every continent, and certain photographic and visual images, from television and the cinema, have found their way across the oceans. When they are transported overseas, has the national authenticity been thereby erased? Have they lost their national identity, or are they coveted elsewhere because of a presumed "American" identity? Is this an easy and accessible way of consuming American culture without acknowledging its inherent ambiguities and complexities?

IV: PEDAGOGY AS IDEOLOGY

Back to the artist, the creator of images to commemorate the traumas and crises. Ever since Gropius set in motion the educational elements of the Bauhaus, as we saw in the previous chapter, there was a pedagogical awareness of and quest for a "general universal," as he called it, namely, a way to communicate in terms that would be understood by humanity as a whole. For the Bauhaus movement, there was also a political element in this pedagogical principle, underscored by socialist and utopian thinking. There is a striking parallel between the Bauhaus movement and the Vienna method at least to the extent that both movements or schools of thought agreed as to the pedagogical significance of visual education, both in providing information as well as in communication. Whether one considers visualization in two-dimensional pictorial displays or in three-dimensional structures, there is a pedagogical commitment that belies a political agenda, however tacit.

But here we shift to the propagandist abuses of such lofty commitments, and also notice the corporate appropriation of abstract visualization. It may be called corporate identity; it may be called symbols that attract viewers and appeal to some of their sensibilities as current and potential consumers of the products that are sold through corporate logos and advertisements, images that sell the identity and the product, that bespeak of quality and integrity, that remind us of ideals not readily apparent in buying an appliance or a vacation. What capitalist, corporate elites and their artistic talents recognize, just like their artistic predecessors, is that words as descriptors are not enough and that naturalistic depiction of their products is not enough either in order to appeal to a higher or deeper psychological facet of viewers as consumers. Perhaps the lesson they teach us, the cultural critics and intellectual pedagogues of this century, is that abstraction might hold the key to cognitive appreciation and decision-making. At the same time, an artwork in the exhibition entitled *Mirroring Evil: Nazi Imagery/Recent Art* at the Jewish Museum in New York in the spring of 2002, that tried to juxtapose and provoke Prada brand name, for example, with a death camp model, upset and challenged the art world and the rest of the community. If we translate concerns and controversies like these into our topic of memory, memorials, and commemorative depictions of the horrors of the past, we might appreciate the power of abstract art, and the way we train artists to deploy it for particular purposes.

Like many other professionalized occupations, art making has become part of the class structure of our culture with definite power relations both external and internal to its membership. Whether we consider museum curators, gallery owners, collectors, and critics, we find the artistic community facing multiple concerns for survival, success, and personal integrity. As we look into the future of this century, we find that the concerns of Greek artists and those of the Renaissance (e.g., glorifying their patrons, portraying a national identity, and inspiring the masses to battle all enemies of the state) have only been amplified over the centuries, not reconciled. Is it possible for artists in general and critics in particular to hold onto their ideals, dreams, and integrity while performing their tasks of building monuments and memorials, for example, within the context of a highly commercialized, technoscientific, and global environment?

Like many other professionalized occupations, art making has become part of the class structure of our culture with definite power relations both external and internal to its membership. As we have argued elsewhere (Sassower and Cicotello 2000), one can go back to biblical accounts of the golden calf or to later periods in Europe under the auspices of the Catholic popes, and appreciate the extent to which artworks were subservient to the powers of the day. Did the producers of the golden calf agree, the sculptors and goldsmiths who melted the jewelry of the people, accept the premise under which it was produced? Were they merely reflecting the sentiments of the restless people who grew impatient awaiting Moses' return from Mount Sinai or a deeper concern with the substitution of current icons and deities for an invisible god?

Similarly, we wonder to what extent the Renaissance artists who accepted commissions to glorify the Catholic Church and its cathedrals believed in the doctrines of the church or were merely using its largesse to feed themselves and their coworkers? Were the popes and some of the leading political leaders who aspired, like the Medicis, to hold that office, the only patrons of the arts? Was an acceptance of a commission an implicit pact to agree with their views and endorse their policies? Since the artistic community, however defined historically, is subservient to political and economic power structures, one can easily appreciate the predicament that artists face: Should they remain silent and complicit, enjoy the protection of the political powers, or rather become critics of whatever regime is in power so as to ferment discontent and bring about change? There is ample evidence from both written records and artistic renditions of the various means deployed by Renaissance artists that they felt compelled to hide their true ideological beliefs in fear of losing commissions, including, for example, DaVinci's homosexuality and his disdain for the war efforts of some of his patrons. When we shift our attention to the internal structures and constituents of the artistic community, we find some interesting tensions as well.

We would like to offer some preparatory comments to help contextualize our analysis. To begin with, we should note at this juncture that our focus will be on the pedagogical elements of the artistic community, because no matter how one defines this community, there is a great deal one can learn about its concerns and commitments in light of its pedagogical institutions.

Secondly, as one can observe in the twentieth century, fascist and democratic regimes were similarly interested in advocating and perpetuating their respective ideological conviction through artistic renditions with mass appeal. Understood as propaganda or as patriotic displays, images of heroic acts of bravery and sacrifice, whether clad in industrial or military uniforms, have been produced around world wars and other political crises in order to mobilize public support and ensure the popularity of the leaders who carry out specific policies, such as the draft, economic belt-tightening, international sanctions, or declaration of war. These historic examples illustrate the conditions under which the artistic community as a whole, however poorly or loosely defined, has had to contend with political powers that regulate the range of their activities and can suspend or eliminate their productions.

Thirdly, unlike the patronage and apprenticeship methods of the Renaissance, in the contemporary context we can consider museum curators, gallery owners, collectors, and critics as several powerful groups who put multiple and divergent pressures on the artistic community in general and individual artists in particular. As we look into the future of this century, we find that the concerns of Greek artists and those of the Renaissance have only been amplified over the centuries, not reconciled. Is it possible for artists to hold onto their ideals, dreams, and integrity while performing their tasks within the context of a highly commercialized, technoscientific, and global environment?

Before we answer this question about the tightrope that artists must walk between complicity and critical authenticity in this particular context, let us lay some groundwork. To begin with, the case of twentieth-century avant-garde artists was fully discussed by us elsewhere (Sassower and Cicotello 2000) so as to account for the success of avant-garde artists, such as Magritte and Warhol, who understood how to be critical and provocative while being able to show and sell their works in the best galleries around the world. There is something uncanny, almost surreal about the maintenance of an aura of personal authenticity with revolutionary zest that is commercially appealing.

But more importantly to the specific area we want to examine here are the ways in which education has been linked to politics. The Brazilian educator Paulo Freire and his local counterpart Henry Giroux have argued forcefully about this link in both theoretical and practical terms. *Pedagogy of the Oppressed* (1970) became the modern benchmark for any such discussions. Of course one can look back to Plato's *Republic* and make similar points about the role of educational indoctrination. The ideals of the state, whether democratic or not, could be passed on from one generation to another through the curriculum. The more formal the ideals, the more formal the teachings and the more pronounced their presence is. Socrates' guardians were to train the youth in their intellectual as well as their physical ways and ensure that the Polis was well guarded and efficiently run. As we move to the twentieth century some things change: the links between our educational system and our political institutions are more remote and seemingly less intrusive (in the sense of overtly pushing for an ideology, even though textbooks are carefully chosen and curricula are heatedly debated). Perhaps the expectation of the training of citizens has taken on a different character in which the hegemony of the state is taken for granted.

Freire demonstrates that the cultural and economic concerns of the political elites are "reproduced" both in the content of the curricula and the manner in which they are presented. There is a strong sense that a critical dimension should be undermined if not completely eliminated; educational institutions are hierarchical, and the classrooms themselves reflect the posture of one leader and many followers who parrot what is taught (Freire 1970). In later treatises, Freire pushed these ideas further and demonstrated the power of movements, such as Liberation Theology in Latin America, are shifting discourses to unintended consequences. Though the opening of theological interpretations could break the lock hold of bishops and priests over their congregants, it could also incite political unrest. Once oppression is recognized, it doesn't matter who the oppressor is in order to mobilize resistance. The president is no better or worse than the priest and the teacher; their position in the social hierarchy bespeaks of unbridled power and therefore ought to be overthrown.

Obviously, in order to make these arguments stick in the context of the United States, we need to be careful in collecting data, examples that illustrate the ways in which capitalist and conservative ideologies find their way into the curriculum, the textbooks, and the classrooms. What do our students read? Who decides what they read? Who decides how they read? Are critical interpretations encouraged, or are they supposed to regurgitate their teachers' pronouncements? We take these to be self-evident questions observed by all of us. Are we indeed reproducing the capitalist working classes so as to ensure a smooth transition from youth to adulthood in the workplace? Are we providing the kind of education that would maintain a docile work force that wouldn't challenge the "bosses" or the structural inequities built into their very existence?

If this sounds Marxist, so be it; if this sounds more Frankfurt-school style, so be it. But we are sure that one could take the course requirements of any business school in this country and map out exactly the kind of professional training Freire is worried about. We are not promoting intellectual curiosity in an open-ended manner so as to cultivate informed citizens; rather we are training professionals to pursue prefigured ideals and fully endorse the economic and social structures already in place. How does this relate to art schools? In a word: there's no difference in principle between engineering, business, law, and art schools: they are all reproducing capitalism.

These questions were on the minds of the founders of the Bauhaus School, from the original inspiration of the Belgian van de Velde to the actual director of the school Walter Gropius. Both the "Manifesto" and the "Programme" focused on the incorporation of the arts and crafts with the world of industrial commerce, so that the benefits of training for particular needs of manufacturers would be the driving force of the interaction, obviously in a manner unfamiliar to the traditional German art academy. Though short in its practice (1919–1932), and though moved from Weimar to Dessau and eventually to Berlin, the movement was responding to the Industrial Revolution of the nineteenth century on the one hand and the outdated pedagogical practices of European art schools whose Romanticism was becoming outdated with the technological developments of the early twentieth century. The pedagogical ideal rested on three main objectives: first, to rescue the arts from their academic isolation and make their development and effects more readily felt in the booming industrial activities of the day; second, to elevate the crafts to the level of the other, more refined arts, or to blur the distinction between the fine and commercial art mediums into an integrated, seamless set of creative and practical artifacts; and third, to have the arts and artists more integrated into the economic web of production, distribution, and consumption of their works.

The Bauhaus leadership and most of its teachers were aware of the state subsidies that were waning with the economic situation in Germany, and therefore sought other forms of funding for their school and their projects. They openly accommodated the financial agendas of their sponsors, realizing that to be left-wing at the time committed them to helping workers earn a decent living on the one hand, and helping consumers afford useful and relatively inexpensive products with functional style.

It is interesting to note in this context Adolf Loos' contention of 1908 that ornamentation was simply a waste of money. He claimed: "If I pay as much for a smooth box as for a decorated one, the difference in labour time belongs to the worker" (Whitford 1984, 20) Put in Marxist terms, the additional labor time expended by the worker is not compensated for by the capitalist who sells to the consumer, and therefore the worker suffers a greater level of exploitation. An aesthetic decision is couched in an economic analysis. And before you know it, an ideological conviction becomes a pedagogical imperative. The ideological commitments of the Bauhaus were not limited to this form of left-wing or Marxist analysis. There was also a deeper concern with abstraction as a form of universal appeal that could eschew the political climate of nationalism fermenting in different regions of Germany. But abstraction, as the Bauhaus learned quickly, could also be considered an ideological weapon in its own right.

It wasn't surprising that the Nazis found the Bauhaus's aesthetics threatening, devoid of national pride of the origins of Aryan superiority or the folk roots of traditional Germanic beauty and authenticity. Being as they were also suspicious of the cozy relationships between the artistic community and capitalist manufacturing and architecture that allowed individual freedoms and aesthetic choices with personal benefits, the Nazis insisted on close supervision of their ideological manifestations in any art form, and worried about the decadence that one could detect in high-art forms. We don't wish to push this example beyond its limited value for us here and illustrate the irony of the tense relationship between the Bauhaus movement and National Socialism and even Soviet Communism, for most of the state-sponsored building for the workers were inspired by if not directly copied from the outlines of the Bauhaus movement.

As for the pedagogical elements found in the Bauhaus art school, we wish to note that the reaction against commercialism of one kind—the one described more fully below—was undertaken with a keen eye on the mutual benefits the artistic and commercial communities could enjoy: funding the one in order to produce the other, recognizing the web of economic entanglements they both must work within in order to enjoy aesthetic and financial success.

Of course, to talk of capitalism is to talk about numerous principles and ideals, and all the different ways in which they are manifested in contemporary culture. Let's outline just a few and connect them to specific pedagogical devices. Each principle is related to all the others, but for the sake of convenience we separate them here:

1. *Competition*—understood negatively as "anything goes" or positively as ambition and motivation, it has been the bedrock of most of the explanatory models regarding the benefits of the capitalist system to the development of human spirit and its work ethics. The notion of competition has been linked to Darwin's principles of natural selection on the one hand and Condorcet's view of the perfectibility of the human mind. Social stratification as well as economic inequalities have been explained away with this basic sense that anyone can strive and work hard, compete in the marketplace for her or his share of success.

In more academic settings this means that students compete against each other, learn how to climb the aesthetic ladder to the heights expected of them. When critiques go on, some get better grades than others, some artworks are valued more favorably than others, some get scholarships and some don't. In some fundamental way we train students to compete rather than cooperate with each other, telling them that we are preparing them for the real world, as if the world in which they live in the moment is somehow unreal. Does that encourage students to hurt each other in order to succeed, steal ideas in order to excel, put down others in order to shine by comparison? Is the artistic pie only so big that everyone must fight everyone else in order to get a slice, as sometimes is said to be the case with the capitalist pie of zero-sum games?

2. *Profit Maximization*—understood invariably in terms of making the best of what you have, taking full advantage of what is available. This notion is also understood in trying to balance one's costs in terms of one's revenue. The ancient custom of bookkeeping remains with us as a way to examine the bottom line, the line that tells us whether there is a loss or profit at the end of the day. When the focus is on profit maximization or optimalization (in more sophisticated economic models), then we might cut corners, limit expenses deemed unnecessary, or be ruthless about how to ensure that profits guide our decision-making processes. Incidentally, this focus contrasts sharply with other economic frameworks that underscore environmental as well as human concerns in the process of production, distribution, and consumption so that if there is a profit or not is secondary to the ways in which humans are treated respectfully and perhaps at greater costs.

In the classroom the notion of profit maximization is translated into how art schools and colleges are organized. Since professional training costs money, and since training can be achieved for less cost if we hire only part-time instructors, or instructors with less academic credentials, then we'll do that instead of lavishing large stipends on highly qualified and expensive alternatives. This is not to say that at times less credentialed instructors might not be much better instructors than more credentialed ones. Rather, this is just an illustration of how administrators are inclined to cut costs regardless of the quality of education. Likewise, classrooms will be designed so as to accommodate more rather than fewer students at a time, studios will be more cramped than is comfortable, all in the name of efficiency and cost saving. It's a fine line between being frugal and efficient and being counterproductive and detrimental to the success of students.

3. *Entrepreneurship*—understood as individualistic pursuit of one's goals and dreams. In the positive sense, this belies self-reliance, self-confidence, and a certain sense of purpose. In the negative sense, this belies a deep sense of loneliness and alienation. There is no sense of community when the lone rider mounts the horse on the quest for fame and fortune in the western horizon. Risk taking comes to mind as well as an appreciation that personal integrity and ingenuity are the only elements one needs to succeed in the world. Obviously, this sense of independence and autonomy is seductive and forms the basis of western civilization. Yet, we ought to remember that the only way entrepreneur-

ship can flourish is if it's set within political and legal frameworks that encourage and protect it. So, however shunned and despised, the community as a whole provides the conditions of success for those pursuing their dreams (whether in terms of tax credits for investments or losses).

In the classroom, once again, students are encouraged to come up with their own ideas, be original, go at it on their own, and display moments of genius. In this way, the history of art, for example, recedes to a faint background to be ignored, rather than the foundation upon which anything new or novel is based. Likewise, the pressure on the individual to see herself or himself alone may do more damage than good. As we said about competition as motivation and ambition, so we can say about rugged individualism, that it might turn friendly encounters into vicious fights over originality and priority.

4. *The Invisible Hand of the Marketplace*—one of the hallmarks of capitalism and the locus of so many discussions about freedom and equality—the two guiding principles of the Enlightenment—the marketplace is where capitalism happens. Anyone is allowed to trade with anyone else anything that comes to mind: goods, services, goodwill, and ideas. The price is determined in the classical literature in terms of supply and demand, the respective quantities of each help establish a fair price for anything that is being bought and sold. What has convinced generations across the western hemisphere that this model is workable is the fact that there are no barriers to entry, as they are called, so anyone can participate equally in the marketplace; anyone can exit it at will; and anyone has a fair chance to succeed under equal conditions. The freedom to participate and the freedom from price controls and governmental interference has been lauded as the best framework to observe freedom; likewise, it's the best model, according to its proponents, to ensure that equal opportunity of competition is not absolute equality in some idealized manner. It should be noted in this context that advocates of neoclassical capitalism, such as Milton Friedman of the Chicago School, have claimed that politics are bound by the economy rather than the other way around. We vote with our wallets: the contributions we make to political candidates and the choices we make with our expenditures are more reliable indicators and reflect more accurately our tastes.

What this means in the academic setting is a bit more complex. We must ask ourselves whether the classroom itself is a marketplace of sorts;

likewise, we must ask ourselves to what extent education is part of the marketplace of ideas or not; finally, we must ask ourselves whether or not the academic marketplace indeed fosters equality and freedom. When the curriculum is set by teachers and administrators, it's unclear how free the environment is; when the academic hierarchy sets up power relations among the participants in the academic marketplace, it's unclear how equal we all are. Outside support is called in to shift the ground of exchange and opinion-brokers: theoretical debate over the "nature" of originality by artists is used by critics in terms of marketing profiles that would bolster their assessments and assertions. But from another standpoint, we could also be concerned about turning the academic environment into a capitalist marketplace: Is everything and everyone indeed for sale? Do we put price tags on everything, including creativity and aesthetic appeal? Are we in fact reproducing artists for the great capitalist machinery so that the wheels of commerce will be lubricated just the right way, and beautifully as well?

5. *Private Property*—one of the salient differences between the socialist ideology and the capitalist relates to the fact that rather than have the state own everything on behalf of and for the benefit of the population, individuals have the right to own property. Government agencies cannot be trusted to own land and buildings, bridges and roads as custodians of the citizenry, because they would accumulate power in the hands of a few rulers and bureaucrats. In commercial terms this has been translated into copyright and trademark licenses, so that people not only own material goods, such as homes and cars, but also own their ideas. A corporate logo and a food recipe are legally protected for the exclusive use and financial benefit of those who developed them. Whether it's the old-fashioned forms of brain power and information, such as books, or the more recent forms of computer knowledge, capitalist formation insists on considering one's brain trust as property with economic value worthy of legal protection.

We wonder how the notion of copyright plays itself out within a tradition that incorporated copying old masters as one of the methods of skill acquisition. We are not concerned with forgery here, namely, the deliberate attempt to profit from misleading a buyer to believe that an art piece is what it's not; rather, we are worried about where to draw the line between teaching art students to copy a piece of art just the way they would observe a model in figure drawing class. Isn't the biggest compliment to one's creation that it has been copied? What do we do with Walter Benjamin's analysis of mechanical reproduction of works of art? Is one's work really private and really a piece of property? When a chef produces an incredible dish and then offers the recipe for free or for a fee, is anyone worried about copying? To what extent have twentieth-century avant-garde artists made "copying" an original art form—as in the case of Sherie Levine's gold-plated urinal in relation to Duchamp's *Fountain*? Is the process of copying not in itself a way of paying homage to the great masters on the one hand, and an act of appropriation and recreation on the other? Incidentally, if we look back at Renaissance artists, similar themes and even techniques are repeatedly reproduced.

It is for all of these historical reasons and their current instantiations that we move our focus to art institutes and schools of art that are supposed to "train" artists. Ours is an analysis of this academic process of training in which the consequences and predicaments of ideological commitments are revealed. We aren't simply saying that "everything is political," but rather underscoring the ways in which curricular components, such as art history, multiculturalism, techniques, as well as portfolio presentations, indirectly disclose ideological convictions and commitments (in the ways in which certain artists are chosen over others in teaching a history class or in the ways in which theoretical frameworks are discussed or assumed to be the appropriate ones for art students). Art pedagogy, then, is political in two related but different ways: on the one hand, its institutional choices reflect broader ideological commitments, from capitalism to hierarchical power relations, from the cult of the genius to group work; and on the other hand, its very existence reflects some ideological commitments on the part of the broader art community.

This in turn is true also in two related but different ways: first, in the sense that artists should or should not be trained within academic confines and what sanctions do they enjoy when graduating; and second, in the sense that art schools are supported by or refuse support from nonprofit private funding organizations, museums and galleries, and federal funding agencies.

V: THE FUTURE OF AESTHETIC PEDAGOGY

Our purpose here is to tease out the predicament of art pedagogy in facing competing political agendas, trying as hard as it can to remain autonomous from ideological squabbles while pandering to individuals and institutions that fund them. Should art professors train students to be political critics or ideological promoters? Will and can they protect them when their criticism earns them public scorn and deliberate exclusion from funding opportunities? When every submission is subject to judgment and in fact a grading scale of sorts, isn't it appropriate for art schools to subject their work to a grade? Shouldn't we all get used to being pegged on some level of an aesthetic ladder whose scale is determined by someone else? The self-evaluaton and self-promotion of our artistic work might seem silly if not downright self-serving if we are to survive in the aesthetic marketplace.

Perhaps in light of these questions and comments, we might be better prepared to answer some fundamental questions regarding pedagogical models for art students. Should they be using the apprenticeship method that is valued in the medical profession so that they become more attuned to the finer nuances of the artistic marketplace? Should their salesmanship and craft be honed by teachers or by practitioners? This dichotomy is obviously a false one, since just like physicians, art teachers are both teachers and practitioners. Yet, when a teacher is guaranteed a fixed income, is there a greater likelihood for experimentation and outright defiance of the commercial marketplace of artworks? Likewise, we could choose a more Socratic method of artistic training so that the very foundations of the techniques of art-making and their various mediums would come under careful scrutiny. Perhaps we can see some of this in performance art or environmental art that reject the museum and gallery as the only venues for public display. But where is the funding? Why has video art become more popular lately than twenty years ago when the technology was already available? If technological innovations drive shifts in technique, there is also a popular market for some artworks and not for others. Young adults of the twenty-first century are more likely to be consumers of video art through television sets, computer screens, and cybercafes than their parents who still feel the bourgeois urge to visit a museum when traveling to a foreign city.

The urgency of these questions not as theoretical exercise but rather as lived realities that have become apparent in light of the war in Iraq and the various pacifist responses to it by artists. What we mean by this in a very limited way is the way in which television networks, such as CNN, have determined the course of action and response by the public and its political and military leaderships in an almost Marxist deterministic, materialistic sense. Has the technology available today determined the course of history? Has our inability to resist some of these developments been directly affected by the facts of media infiltration into the lives of our students in and out of the classroom? Can we imagine returning to the days of the old academy model where, like a cloister or a convent, apprentices were deliberately secluded from worldly influences, technological or not?

And if the answer is not, then we must embrace the technologies out there and appropriate them in order to bring about and highlight the tensions that remain between the complicity and critique of artists and their works in relation to the ideological framework within which they work. We should note in closing that there is almost an envious position that underground and dissident artists of totalitarian regimes enjoy, since the "other," the enemy of popular and free thinking, is blatantly evil in its constrains and oppression. By contrast, artists living in democratic regimes, such as our own, face an insidious other or enemy, the one that lets you hang yourself with your work, when no one will buy it because it seems unpatriotic to criticize the war in Iraq or the president of the United States. Yes, all submissions are welcome, but not all are equal in the eyes of the ideological lord.

30

31

32

33

34

35

36

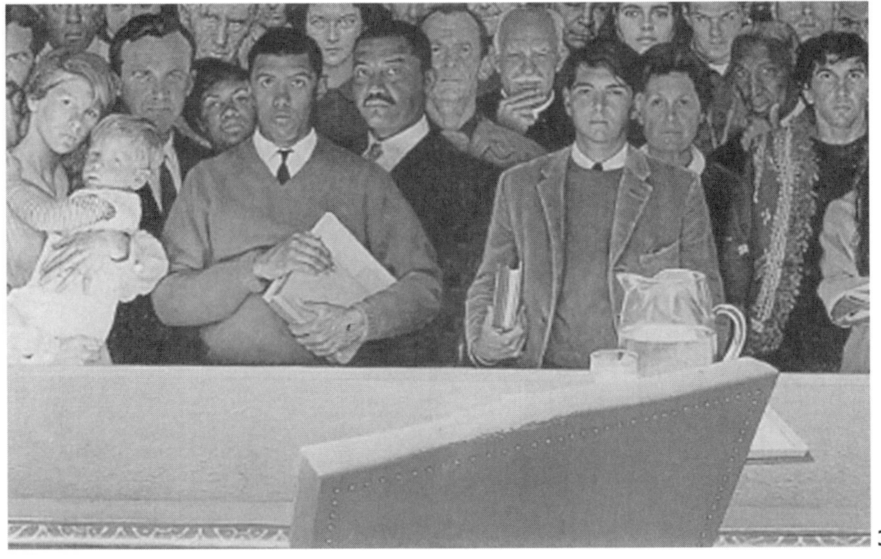

37

BIBLIOGRAPHY

Adorno, Theodor W. 1994. "Anti-Semitism and Fascist Propaganda," in *Adorno: The Stars Down to Earth*. Edited by Stephen Crook. London and New York: Routledge, 135–61.

Bell, Daniel. 1961. *The End of Ideology: On the Exhaustion of Political Ideas in the Fifties*. New York: Collier Books.

Berger, John. 1972. *Ways of Seeing*. London: Penguin.

Bogart, Michele H. 1995. *Artists, Advertising, and the Borders of Art* Chicago and London: The University of Chicago Press.

Boime, Albert. 1991. *The Magisterial Gaze: Manifest Destiny and American Landscape Painting c. 1830–1865*. Washington, DC: The Smithsonian Institution Press.

Buck-Morss, Susan. 1995. "Envisioning Capital: Political Economy on Display," in *Visual Display: Culture Beyond Appearances*. Edited by Lynne Cooke and Peter Wollen, 111–153. Seattle: Bay Press.

Carroll, Noel. 2004. "Art and Human Nature." *The Journal of Aesthetics and Art Criticism* 62, no. 2: 95–107.

Chomsky, Noam. 2000. *New Horizons in the Study of Language and the Mind*. Cambridge: Cambridge University Press.

Clifford, James. 1988. *The Predicament of Culture: Twentieth-Century Ethnography, Literature, and Art*. Cambridge and London: Harvard University Press.

Cohen, Carl, ed. 1972/1962. *Communism, Fascism, and Democracy: The Theoretical Foundations*. New York: Random House.

———. 1982. *Four Systems: Individualist Democracy, Socialist Democracy, Fascism, Communism.* New York: Random House.

Craven, David. 1997. *Diego Rivera as Epic Modernist.* New York: G. K. Hall.

Dahl, Robert. 2003. *How Democratic is the American Constitution?* 2nd ed. New Haven: Yale University Press.

de Sousa, Ronald. 2004. "Is Art Adaptation? Prospects for an Evolutionary Perspective on Beauty." *The Journal of Aesthetics and Art Criticism* 62, no. 2: 109–18.

Dewey, John. 1958. *Art as Experience.* New York: Capricon Books.

Downs, Linda, ed. 1986. *Diego Rivera: A Retrospective.* New York: W. W. Norton.

Eagleton, Terry. 1990. *The Ideology of the Aesthetic.* Oxford and Cambridge, MA: Basil Blackwell.

———. 1991. *Ideology: An Introduction.* London and New York: Verso.

Fauchereu, Serge, ed. 1988. *Moscow: 1900–1930.* New York: Rizzoli.

Fiedler, Jeannine, and Peter Feierabend, eds. 1999. *Bauhaus.* Cologne: Konemann.

Fischer, Ernst. 1959. *The Necessity of Art.* Middlesex: Penguin Books.

Freire, Paulo. 1970. *Pedagogy of the Oppressed.* Translated by Myra Bergman Ramos. New York: Herder and Herder.

Gibson, J. J. 1966. *The Senses Considered as Perceptual Systems.* Boston: Houghton Mifflin.

Gombrich, Ernest. 1961. *Art and Illusion.* Princeton: Princeton University Press.

Goodman, Nelson. 1976. *Languages of Art.* Indianapolis: Hackett.

Guptill, Arthur L. 1946. *Norman Rockwell: Illustrator.* New York: Watson-Guptill.

Hanson, Norwood R. 1958. *Patterns of Discovery.* Cambridge: Cambridge University Press.

Hahn, Peter. 2002. *Bauhaus: 1919–1933.* Koln: Taschen (Bauhaus-Archiv Museum).

Horkheimer, Max, and Theodor W. Adorno. 2002. *Dialectic of Enlightenment: Philosophical Fragments.* Edited by Gunzelin Schmid Noerr and translated by Edmund Jephcott. Stanford: Stanford University Press.

Josephson, Susan G. 1996. *From Idolatry to Advertising: Visual Art and Contemporary Culture.* London: M. E. Sharpe.

Lewontin, R. C. 1991. *Biology as Ideology: The Doctrine of DNA.* New York: HarperCollins.

Macpherson, C. B. 1962. *The Political Theory of Possessive Individualism.* London, Oxford, New York: Oxford University Press.

Marling, Karal Ann. 1997. *Norman Rockwell.* New York: Harry N. Abrams.

Marx, Karl. 1988. *The Communist Manifesto* [1872]. Edited by Fred Bender. New York: W. W. Norton.

Menen, Aubrey. 1980. *Art & Money: An Irreverent History*. New York: McGraw-Hill.

Neurath, Otto. 1973. *Empiricism and Sociology.* Edited by Marie Neurath and Robert S. Cohen. Dodrecht and Boston: Reidel, (especially chapter 7).

Paxton, Robert O. 2005. *The Anatomy of Fascism*. New York: Vintage.

Pound, Ezra. 1996. *Machine Art & Other Writings: The Lost Thought of the Italian Years*. Durham, NC: Duke University Press.

Rockwell, Norman. 1979. *Norman Rockwell: My Adventures as an Illustrator.* Indianapolis: Curtis Publishing Co.

Rosenberg, Donna. 1994. *World Mythology*. New York: McGraw-Hill.

Sassower, Raphael, and Louis Cicotello. 2000. *The Golden Avant-Garde*. Charlottesville: University of Virginia Press.

Thau Heyman, Therese. 1998. *Posters: American Style*. New York: Harry N. Abrams.

Timmers, Margaret, ed. 1998. *The Power of the Poster*. London: V&A Publications.

Walton, Donald. 1978, *A Rockwell Portrait: An Intimate Biography.* Kansas City: Sheed, Andrews, and McMeel.

White, Stephen. 1988. *The Bolshevik Poster*. New Haven: Yale University Press.

Whitford, Frank. 1984. *Bauhaus.* London: Thames & Hudson.

Wittgenstein, Ludwig. 1922. *Tractatus Logico-Philosophicus*. London: Routledge & Kegan Paul.

———. 1958. *Philosophical Investigations*. Translated by G. E. M. Anscombe. New York: Macmillan.

INDEX

ABOUT THE AUTHORS

Raphael Sassower is professor and chair of philosophy at the University of Colorado, Colorado Springs. He is the author most recently of *Confronting Disaster: An Existential Response to Technoscience* (Lexington Books 2004), and with Louis Cicotello *The Golden Avant-Garde: Idolatry, Commercialism, and Art* (Virginia 2000). His research focus is on postmodern technoscience as it relates to a variety of cultural areas, such as aesthetics, pedagogy, and medicine.

Louis Cicotello is professor and former chair of visual and performing arts at the University of Colorado, Colorado Springs. In addition to collaborating with Raphael Sassower on *The Golden Avant-Garde*, he has been a prolific visual artist, exhibiting collages, assemblages, theatrical sets, and sculptures nationwide. His artworks exemplify the artistic predicament of cultural critique. The collage for the cover of this book was designed by him.